Navigating College

A Handbook on Self Advocacy
Written for Autistic Students
from Autistic Adults

First Edition December 2012

ISBN-13: 978-1-938800-00-9

Library of Congress Cataloging-in-Publication Data has been applied for.

Contributions by

Alexander Eveleth

Jim Sinclair

Lydia Brown

Steven Kapp

Amanda Vivian

Leah Jane Grantham

Samantha April Davis

Zoe Gross

Edited and compiled by ASAN Staff Members
Elesia Ashkenazy and Melody Latimer

Illustrations by
Noranne Kramer

Cover design by
Sara Schneider

Indexing by
Paula Durbin-Westby

This resource was funded as part of a grant from the Administration on Developmental Disabilities for the creation of the Autism NOW Resource and Information Center.

Table of Contents

Foreword

Ari Ne'eman

This book was not written for parents. Nor was it written for doctors, teachers, service-providers or any other kind of professional. ASAN welcomes those readers, and we hope they'll learn a thing or two from this resource. Still, I felt it was valuable to begin with that clarification. Too often, autism-related books start from the assumption that most readers will be family members or service-providers of Autistic people, rather than individuals on the spectrum. Despite an unprecedented level of public awareness of the autism spectrum over the course of the last decade, the national conversation about autism has usually been about Autistic people, without Autistic people. We're trying to change that. As a result, the authors of this book are adults and youth on the autism spectrum writing primarily for an Autistic audience. So, to any of our readers from the parent and professional communities, please do keep reading—but when you're done, consider what you can do to get a copy into the hands of the Autistic people in your life.

This book is written for current and future Autistic college students. In our society, the words "autism" and "college" often seem not to go well together. When I was going through high school, I frequently had to argue with my school's special education system about what I could expect after I graduated. I saw college in my future—they were much less sure. Although my parents were a lot more supportive, they had a lot of anxiety about my moving to another state to attend school. Some of you may have gone through similar experiences growing up. Others may have had the opposite experience, trying to deal with school systems and family members who don't want to accept your need for accommodations or even the fact that you are Autistic at all. No matter what kind of expectations you faced before going to college, the likelihood is that you will be attending a campus that has not given a great deal of thought to the idea that people like us are going to be a part of it.

Although there are some college programs geared specifically for students on the autism spectrum, they are of varying levels of quality, and most of you will be going to college without any specialized autism program. That's okay though—we wrote this handbook because we believe that being Autistic shouldn't close any doors for you when deciding to pursue higher education. Whether you're at a school with an autism support program or one that offers only a very basic disability services office, this handbook should be a valuable resource in trying to figure out how to make college a positive experience for you. For students with many other kinds of differences, there are a lot of resources available at their campus. Your school may have a Women's Center, a Multi-Cultural Center, a GLBTQ Center, and any number of other diversity-oriented programs, activities and clubs. While there are a few colleges that now have disability pride clubs and/or Disability Cultural Centers, most do not offer those sorts of opportunities. Maybe you'll be the one to start some of these things on your campus. Until then, though, we've created this handbook to make sure that you have someplace to turn when questions arise.

There are a lot of autism resources out there and even a few ones relating to autism and higher education. Although there are certainly a lot of flaws in this genre, many of these publications are still very useful, and I encourage you to take advantage of them should you find one that fits your needs. Still, this book is different in some important ways. It is written by Autistic people ourselves rather than professionals or family members. This distinction is key—we know our own needs better than those who speak for and to us.

In addition, this book is focused on more than just succeeding in the classroom. While classes and homework are important parts of college, no one tries to tell non-disabled students that this is the totality of their college experience. Clubs, social activities, dormitory life, parties, sex and relationships and countless other things should take up at least as much of your waking hours as schoolwork does. For those of you who will be living on campus, and even for many of you who will not be, college isn't just a place to go to take courses—it is a way of life. We'd be doing you a disservice if we didn't talk about the parts of the college experience that happen outside of the classroom.

While writing this guide, we worked to remember that growing up Autistic encompasses a lot of different experiences. Some of us were in the special education system, others received no services. Some of us were in inclusive classrooms—others were in separate classes or schools. Although an increasing number of Autistic youth grow up knowing about our diagnoses, a significant portion of our community discover their Autistic identity in adulthood—sometimes from a doctor, sometimes from parents or family members and sometimes from one's own internal recognition. And let's not leave out the many ways in which we are different that have nothing to do with our diagnosis—we Autistic folks come from every possible background. Whether we're talking about race, religion, gender, sexual orientation, ethnic origin, language, other disability status or countless other ways of reflecting identity, the Autistic experience in this country includes all forms of diversity. We've endeavored to reflect that in this handbook. We realize we may not always succeed—and expect that further editions will need to be added to and revised to ensure we capture perspectives and experiences that were left out. Nonetheless, this is an important beginning for our community. After decades of only being able to turn to resources written by others, we can finally begin to construct support systems for each other, which more accurately reflect our priorities, needs and experiences.

A few final pieces of advice before you set out to read this handbook: First, know that the information you read here may provide you with different advice than you've gotten from your parents or relatives. That's okay. One of the most important realizations you can make as you become an adult is that there is nothing wrong with making decisions that others disagree with. Our family members are frequently our strongest allies—but part of growing up is making choices, even and especially those that are different from the choices that other people would make for us. College is a time for that transition to occur. It is a time for new experiences, testing boundaries and breaking rules. It can be a dangerous time—but that danger is part of the experience. Risk—and the right to choose to take it on—is a necessary part of becoming an adult.

Second, understand that the "safety net" in college is considerably weaker than what you may be used to in high school. As Jim Sinclair explains in his introduction, there are very different expectations under the laws and protections that apply to students with disabilities in K-12 school system as compared to those that apply to students with disabilities who are in higher education settings. Whereas in high school, the school district possessed a responsibility to provide you with a "free and appropriate public education" in the least restrictive environment, in college your school is only obligated to provide accommodations to ensure equal access. In addition, the responsibility shifts to you to make the request for accommodations, rather than having your parents or your teachers make it for you. That's a big change. We're hoping that this book can make that change a little easier for you.

Finally, at the risk of sounding cliché, don't forget to have fun! In this book, there's a lot of advice dealing with the challenges and obstacles you'll face when going to college. Still, at the end of the day, college can and should be a very rewarding experience. It will open a lot of doors for you and give you a chance to define who you want to be. That's worth being excited about. The reason we're paying so much attention getting you through the obstacles you might encounter is so that you can get to the exciting part sooner—because we believe that college is something everyone should have an opportunity to experience, regardless of neurology.

So I welcome you, not just to the ASAN Navigating College handbook, but to the college experience as a whole. It can be a wild ride—but it is one well worth experiencing. Make use of this handbook to help guide you through some of the difficult parts—and don't hesitate to e-mail ASAN at info@autisticadvocacy.org if you have questions about any issues that this handbook doesn't cover. Remember: at the end of the day, your identity as an Autistic person and as a college student is what you decide it should mean. Who we are should not need to be a barrier to experiencing the things this world has to offer. As you embark upon your college journey, know that others like you have traversed this same path—and that no matter what lies ahead, we'll be behind you, backing you up every step of the way.

—Ari Ne'eman, ASAN President

Introduction

Jim Sinclair

If you're reading this guide, chances are you're an autistic student who is attending college, or about to start college soon, or perhaps you're still in high school and thinking ahead to college. You have succeeded, or expect to succeed, in earning a high school diploma. Perhaps you've already applied to and been accepted by the college or university of your choice. Or you may be just starting to think about applying.

Wherever you are in the college process, it will help you to understand some important differences between what you've experienced in high school and what you can expect to experience in college. The rights and responsibilities of college students are very different from those of students in elementary and high school.

The Laws

The American federal law protecting the rights of disabled elementary and secondary school students is the Individuals with Disabilities Education Act (IDEA). Very briefly, if you are a student with a disability in elementary or high school, your public school district must allow you to enroll in school. It's not allowed to reject you on the grounds that your disability would prevent you from mastering the regular curriculum. It is required to assess your support needs and to provide you with an Individualized Education Program (IEP) that includes the supports and services you need in order to learn. Your IEP might include non-academic services such as physical, occupational, or speech therapy, independent living skills training, vocational education, and behavioral support, in addition to academic support in the classroom. If, even with extra supports and services, you are not able to access the regular curriculum and/or function in the regular classroom, the district is required to educate you with an individually adapted curriculum and/or in an alternate environment (the least restrictive environment possible for you).

For more information about IDEA and the rights of elementary and high school students with disabilities, and resources for self-advocacy by students still in high school, see:

http://nichcy.org/wp-content/uplo ads/docs/st1.pdf

http://fvkasa.org/resources/files/ed-advocating-hsms.php

http://nichcy.org/laws/idea

Once you leave high school and apply to or enroll in college, you are no longer covered by the IDEA. The laws that protect disabled college students are the Americans with Disabilities Act (ADA) and Section 504 of the Rehabilitation Act of 1973. These laws prohibit public institutions (including most colleges and universities) from discriminating against "otherwise qualified" individuals on the basis of disability.

Specifically regarding colleges and universities, this means that a college is allowed to set standards for who is "qualified" to be accepted as a student, and to reject applicants who do not meet those standards. It's just not allowed to reject an applicant who does meet the requirements, based solely on the fact that the applicant has a disability.

(Some colleges and universities offer special non-degree programs especially for students with disabilities. Those programs may have different standards for qualified students. They may accept disabled students who do not have high school diplomas, or who have low grade point averages in high school. They may offer special classes only for disabled students, or they may permit disabled students to attend regular classes with modified assignments or grading.)

There are also some colleges especially for autistic or learning-disabled students, that offer traditional academic degree programs along with additional disability-specific services.

Either of these kinds of programs may provide individualized supports such as educational coaches and life skills training. But colleges and universities are not required to offer this kind of special program.

The rest of this section is about the legal rights of students, and requirements for colleges and universities, in traditional degree programs at colleges that are not

specifically for students with disabilities.

For more information about postsecondary education specifically for students with intellectual and developmental disabilities, see:

http://www.thinkcollege.net/

Your Rights and Responsibilities Under the ADA and Section 504

Once a qualified student with a disability has been accepted by a college, the college is required to provide reasonable academic accommodations and modifications to provide the student with equal access to the educational program. It is important to realize that the accommodations and modifications required in college are much less extensive than the services required for high school students under IDEA. Some of the important differences to consider are:

Student's responsibility for notification and documentation.

In college, it is the student's responsibility to inform the appropriate office (usually an office that's called something like Disability Support Services) of a disability that requires accommodation. It is the student's responsibility to provide documentation of the disability and to request accommodations. It is the student's responsibility to deliver accommodations letters to faculty, and to self-advocate with faculty to make sure the accommodations are received. If the student does not self-identify, document the disability, and request accommodations, the college is not required to seek out that student and offer any special services. If a professor does not provide the accommodations the student is entitled to receive, it is the student's responsibility to report this to the ADA/Section 504 Compliance Officer. The college does not monitor faculty to make sure they comply with students' accommodations letters.

What this means for you:
Deciding to disclose

It's up to you to decide whether you wish to disclose your disability and request accommodations. Some students decide not to disclose, and to do without disability-related accommodations. There is some risk to this, in that if you do not request accommodations for your disability, and you end up failing a class or getting a poor grade due to your disability, you cannot request that accommodations be made retroactively. You can decide to disclose your disability and request accommodations at any time, but those accommodations will only be in effect from the time you make the request. They won't undo the poor grade you received before you requested the accommodations.

Required documentation:

If you decide to request accommodations, you should make an appointment with the disability support office. You should bring up-to-date documentation of your disability and of your functional limitations—the impact your disability has on your ability to function in college.

If you had an IEP in high school, it would be helpful to bring a copy of your latest IEP, but that alone is not enough. A letter from a doctor or psychologist documenting your diagnosis is not enough either. Your most recent triennial evaluation would be very helpful, if it was completed within the last three years. Otherwise, you should request an updated report from a doctor or psychologist that details your functional limitations.

If the doctor or psychologist suggests particular accommodations that would help you in college, he or she should clearly explain how those suggested accommodations relate to the limitations that are caused by your disability.

Accommodations letter
The disability support staff will work with you to write an accommodations letter, which you will be responsible for giving to each of your professors. Most accommodations letters are fairly vague about the nature of the disability. They read something like, "This is to inform you that <student's name> has a disability and is entitled to reasonable accommodations under Section 504 and the Americans with Disabilities Act," and then list the accommodations the professor should provide.

It may, or may not, be in your interest to give your professors, college administrators, and/or fellow students more information about the nature of your disability. This is your decision to make. The documentation you provide to the disability support office is confidential. They will not disclose it to anyone else without your written consent (except in exceptional circumstances where information-sharing may be required by law).

Compliance
Most college professors are happy to provide reasonable accommodations once they receive the required information in an accommodations letter. Occasionally a faculty member has concerns about the reasonableness or fairness of a requested accommodation, or believes that the request violates

the professor's academic freedom. If this happens to you, you should first try to negotiate directly with the professor if possible. Explain that the purpose of the accommodations is to allow you to learn the material that the professor wants to teach. Listen to the professor's concerns, and try to find a reasonable way to meet both your and the professor's needs. Be polite and respectful, but do not sacrifice your own rights.

It is usually a good idea for an autistic student to have an advocate present during this kind of discussion with a professor. But as much as possible, you should speak for yourself rather than sit passively and let your advocate speak for you.

It's also important to have a "paper trail" documenting your communications with faculty and administrators. You should request meetings in writing, explaining your concerns that you wish to discuss during the meeting. After a meeting, you should follow up with a written summary of what was discussed and decided at the meeting. Be sure to keep copies of your memos or emails about your accommodation needs.

If communicating directly with the professor is not effective, then ask the disability support office for help. Your college should also have a compliance officer whose job is to make sure the college does not violate the ADA or Section 504. If the disability support office is unable to help you resolve the problem, your next step is to complain to the compliance officer.

If you are not able to resolve the problem by working with administrators at your college, you may file a complaint with the Department of Justice. Be aware that this is a long, drawn-out process, and even if the

Department of Justice eventually decides in your favor, the remedy might only be a requirement for the college to change its procedures in the future. It might not help you much, if at all. Filing a formal complaint should be a last resort, only if you are unable to work things out directly with the college.

Essential requirements of the program of study

In college, if a student cannot fulfill the requirements of the course of study, even with reasonable accommodations and modifications, the student can be dismissed for failing to make satisfactory academic progress. The college is not obliged to make any modifications to the essential requirements of the program.

What this means for you:

You should make a realistic assessment of the requirements of the course of study, your own ability to meet those requirements, and what accommodations and support you would need in order to meet them.

Do not expect the college to waive essential requirements that other students are required to meet. Instead, work with the disability support office to explore any support services and reasonable accommodations that may make it possible for you to meet those requirements.

Some possible accommodations you can expect the college to provide, if you can document your need for them, are:

- Note takers in class, so you don't have to split your attention between listening to lectures and writing down notes.

- Copies of visual aids the professor shows during class.

- Extra time for taking exams.

- Taking exams in a separate and less distracting environment, away from the rest of the class. (If fluorescent lighting is a problem for you, be sure to request a room with non-fluorescent lighting for exams.)

- Receiving course materials in alternate format (electronic files or audio recordings) if you have difficulty reading text.

- Minor modifications to assignments or exams.

- Sometimes autistic or learning disabled students receive extra time to complete assignments and projects. However, this can very easily backfire if you end up falling further and further behind with a growing number of unfinished assignments as you approach the end of the term. A more helpful and effective accommodation might be—

- Reduced course load—taking fewer classes than a typical full-time student, so you can spend more time on each class, and keep up with your assignments. Taking fewer courses at a time also means fewer shifts in attention between different courses, which is often a more autistic-friendly arrangement.

- Occasionally, and only if a course is not considered an essential requirement to a program of study, you might be allowed to substitute a different course for one that your disability makes particularly difficult for you.

Student Code of Conduct

In college, if a student violates the student conduct code, the college is not required to provide a functional behavior assessment, any behavior intervention or support services, or educational services in an alternate environment. A student whose disability prevents him or her from complying with the conduct code is not considered to be an "otherwise qualified" student, and is subject to the same disciplinary procedures as nondisabled students, up to and including expulsion.

What this means for you: It is your responsibility to manage your own behavior and to make sure you comply with the student conduct code.

While most autistic college students are able to conduct themselves responsibly without running afoul of conduct codes, a small number of autistic students have unfortunately created some negative impressions among college faculty and administrators. Based on the communications I've personally seen, the most common conduct complaints about autistic students seem to be "disruptive" behavior in the classroom (often this means making too many comments or asking too many questions, or otherwise distracting the professor and the other students), outbursts or meltdowns in the classroom or elsewhere on campus, and inappropriate expressions of sexuality.

You should read your college's code of student conduct, make sure you understand it, and if you have any reason to think you may need help to comply with it, arrange to get that assistance in place before you start college!

Some suggestions for avoiding the most common kinds of problems for autistic college students:

- To avoid distracting the class with too many questions or comments, limit your in-class participation to two or three brief questions/comments per class session. If you have more questions or comments than that, write down your ideas. Email them to the professor later, or ask to meet with the professor during his or her office hours to discuss them. Better yet, research the questions on your own, and then show the professor what you find out. Professors don't generally appreciate having over-eager students hijack their classroom lectures, but they do appreciate having students who express interest and curiosity about their subjects! By communicating your questions and comments to the professor outside of class, via email or meetings during office hours, you can turn your intense autistic focus into an asset instead of having it seen as a "behavior problem."

- If you are prone to meltdowns (or shutdowns, which are less "disruptive" but can also be problematic and even dangerous), develop your own self-management plan before you start college. If you needed a paraprofessional to help you control your behavior in high school, ask the disability support office to help you identify resources for hiring an assistant for yourself at college. (As explained below in item 4, the college will not provide an assistant for you, as this is considered a personal service. But the disability support staff might be able to refer you to other agencies to help recruit and/or pay for an aide.) Identify stressors and triggers that put you at risk of meltdown or shutdown, and plan ways to avoid or deal with those situations. Some possible strategies might be:

- scheduling "down time" between classes instead of having one class right after another;

- having a designated "safe place" or "crash space" on campus where you can go to be alone if you need to decompress;

- avoiding loud areas, crowds, stimulating activities, or anxiety-provoking meetings at times when you are already stressed; requesting (with appropriate documentation) a private room if you are living on campus, to avoid the extra challenges of dealing with a roommate; or if your college requires students to live on campus but you would find that too stressful, requesting (again, with appropriate documentation) an exemption from this requirement, so you can live at home with your family and commute to college;

- bringing an advocate or facilitator with you to potentially confusing or difficult administrative meetings;

- checking in as needed with a trusted friend or mentor who can help you with relaxation techniques.

Social relationships

Social relationships in general, and sexual relationships in particular, are complicated even for neurotypical people. Autistic young adults often get into difficulty due to misreading cues and misunderstanding expectations. Traditional social skills instruction for autistic people tends to stress emulating neurotypical behavior. Unfortunately, this approach puts autistic people at an inherent disadvantage and fails to tap into autistic strengths. I recommend instead that autistic people (and NT people who are involved in any way with autistic people) cultivate a strong sense of boundaries and evaluate social behaviors in functional terms. Specifically:

- Be very careful not to violate anyone else's personal boundaries. Pay special attention to definitions of sexual harassment, and scrupulously avoid doing anything that falls within or even close to those definitions.

- Be equally careful to protect your own personal boundaries. Autistic people who are desperate for acceptance and friendship, or who are simply naïve about social expectations, often fall prey to people who manipulate and exploit them by pretending to be friends. Remember that real friends are people who respect your boundaries and treat you with respect. A person who tries to invade your boundaries or who makes you feel inferior is not your friend.

- Besides being careful of your own and other people's personal boundaries, also be careful that you are not interfering with other people's ability to go about their own business.

- Be clear about distinctions between mandatory and voluntary interactions. Mandatory things are those you must do in order to succeed in college, whether you want to or not. For example, if you want to earn passing grades, you need to show up for class. Voluntary things are those you don't have to do if you don't want to, even if everyone else is doing them. For example, if your department is having a holiday party, and you don't like parties, you don't have to go.

- If you are not violating anyone's boundaries, are not interfering with anyone else's business, and are meeting your mandatory obligations as a student, you can reasonably assert a right to behave in ways that others may consider strange or weird (including opting out of things that most other people are doing).

- If people ask you why you are doing something they may consider weird, this is one of the circumstances in which it can be helpful to disclose your autism and explain how the "weird" behavior is functional for you. For example, you can explain why you don't make normal eye contact, how a person can tell that you're paying attention if you're not making eye contact, how stimming helps you maintain your equilibrium, how perseveration helps you stay focused and get things done, that you find noisy crowded parties overwhelming but are happy to spend time with one or two people at a time, etc.

- Be aware that even non-autistic college students often get carried away with new social experiences to the point that it interferes with their academic focus, leading to poor grades and sometimes dropping out of college. Splitting focus and juggling different priorities is even more difficult for autistic people. Consider what your own priorities are, and avoid getting caught up in too many distractions from your goals.

- Do not expect to have a "normal" social life, and try not to worry too much about whether you have enough friends or someone to date. Autistic people have autistic relationships, which are very unique and special and take a lot more work. Use your time in college to learn and practice general skills in communicating and getting along with other people, understanding yourself and your autistic skills and needs, and, of course, getting a good education! When an opportunity for genuine friendship or romance does come along, that practice will serve you well.

Reasonable accommodations vs. personal services

A college is required to provide reasonable accommodations in order to make its programs accessible to students with disabilities, but is not required to provide personal services.

Some of the services which disabled students may be provided in high school, but are not required to be provided by colleges, include:

- individual therapies (occupational therapy, speech therapy, etc.);

- individual tutoring (although some colleges have tutoring available for any student who needs it, regardless of disability);

- classroom aides for non-academic purposes such as self-care, carrying and handling items, or managing behavior; transportation to and from school;

- assistance with or instruction about activities of daily living;

- facilitation of peer social interactions;

- most other activities or functions that occur outside the classroom. If a student needs these kinds of personal services in order to succeed in college, the student needs to make his or her own arrangements to get the services.

What this means for you:

If you need additional assistance that is considered a personal service, the disability support office might be able to refer you to another agency to get that service. But do not expect the college to provide the service for you. For example, if you have a documented need for a classroom aide, it is a reasonable accommodation for the college to permit the aide to come to class with you, even though the aide is not registered as a student. But the college does not have to hire or train an aide. It is your responsibility to find and pay the aide, or to work with another agency (for example, your state Vocational Rehabilitation agency) to get funding for the aide.

For more information about your rights in college under the ADA and Section 504, see:

http://fvkasa.org/resources/files/ed-college.php

http://fvkasa.org/resources/files/ed-succeed.php

http://www.educationquest.org/transition-to-college/

College is For Adults

This may seem obvious, but elementary and high school students are expected to be "children," and college students are expected to be adults. If you are still in high school, even if you are 18, 19, or 20 years old, look at your IEP forms. Chances are you are still referred to as a "child" on those forms, and your parents are still expected to represent you at your IEP meetings, even though the law requires the school to inform you of the rights that transfer to you when you turn 18. For autistic students, there's also a good chance that well-meaning parent/family advocates will advise parents to seek guardianship when the student turns 18.

When a student is in college, college personnel expect that student to be an independent, responsible adult. They expect the student to advocate for him- or herself; to attend and participate in meetings about his or her academic program, progress, and accommodations; and to make his or her own decisions. In particular, disability support staff tend not to appreciate being called by students' parents about the student's needs.

What this means for you:

If your parents are supportive of your independence, ask them to help you prepare and rehearse for meetings at college.

You can discuss things with them and ask them for advice if you're not sure about something. Your parents can absolutely continue to be supports for you.

But it's not your parents' job to work with the college. You should be the one who actually meets with the college staff. If you need an advocate or facilitator to help you during the meetings, ask someone who is not your parent or other family member to come with you. A Center for Independent Living might be a good place to find an advocate.

Resources on Campus

Even though colleges are not required to provide disability-specific personal services, autistic students may benefit from many services that are available for all students at the colleges. Most colleges have some or all of the following services available:

- Academic advising to help with exploring career interests and possible majors.

- Coaching in study skills and time management.

- Tutoring in academic subjects.

- Help with career planning, preparing resumes, and practicing for job interviews.

- Resident Assistants to assist with housing/roommate issues for students living on campus.

- A counseling center for students experiencing stress, anxiety, social problems, or difficulty adjusting to college life. (Be aware, though, that many counselors do not have experience working with autistic clients. If you feel you need help and the counselors at your college aren't able to help you, ask them to refer you to an outside counselor who understands the needs of autistic clients.)

- Student organizations may be sources of social support and advocacy.

- Informal networking with other students can help with finding mentors and study buddies.

You can learn about these and other services through your college's Office of Student Life.

Resources Outside The College

Your state Vocational Rehabilitation agency may provide funding for disability-related personal services that are not provided by the college, such as personal assistants in or outside the classroom, transportation to school, and assistive technology. Look for the Vocational Rehabilitation agency under your state's Department of Education.

Centers for Independent Living can provide advocacy, independent living skills training, and social contact with disabled peers. You can find out about CILs near you at:

http://www.ilru.org/html/publications/directory/index. html

Online forums can help with information-sharing, networking, and practical tips. Some good autism-specific forums are:

Autistic Daily Living
http://www.yahoo
groups.com/group/autisticdailyliving

University Students with Autism & Asperger's Syndrome
http://www.users.dircon.co.uk/~cns/
and of course

Autistic Self Advocacy Network
http://www.autisticadvocacy.org

Worth

Samantha April Davis

You're a college student now. Things are different from what you are used to. A lot is being asked of you and it's not always easy meeting expectations. Nobody said it was going to be easy. You might have a bit of trouble along the way. You might struggle. A lot of people struggle. You might have to ask for help. You might have to ask even when you feel that you shouldn't have to.

You're in college now. Remember one thing: You made it to college because you have potential. You are in college because you demonstrated capability to get here. If you are struggling now, it is because you are able and, while your needs may be different or beyond that of the typical college student, you are capable of meeting those challenges given proper support.

Higher Education Transitions

Steven Kapp

You have many considerations when planning for what college to attend. One includes whether you begin in community college. Many students begin in community college after high school and transfer to a four-year college or university to save money, allow more time to choose what program they would like to study, or because they do not feel prepared yet for a four-year college. If you do not have qualifications (such as grades, test scores, extracurricular activities, recommendations, and essays) to get into the colleges of your choice directly from high school, earning strong grades in community college allows you another opportunity to apply to a higher program. Students do not usually live on community college campuses, so if you would like to live away from home in college but not feel ready yet straight from high school, you might consider first going to community college and living with your family while practicing daily living skills like doing your own laundry. If you go to a college close to your family, you might go home on the weekends to do such chores or errands too. While I did not go to a community college because I got into and felt ready for most of my top choices among four-year schools, if this did not happen or if I could not afford it, I would have strongly considered beginning in community college. If you do go to community college, try to take classes that will transfer to four-year colleges of interest to you so you can get credit for them there.

Nevertheless, you do not need to know what you want to study before choosing to attend a four-year college. In general I think a wise choice for an academic program matches your interests and abilities, and ideally also offers strong career opportunities. You might consider both the quality (such as ranking, reputation, or particular emphases that interest you) and quantity (such as number and variety of majors and minors) of academic programs. I chose a college that had excellent programs in the two fields that most interested me but also a wide selection of many other programs because I might change my mind and switch. Many if not most college students begin without a declared major or switch majors, and my planning process allowed me to become one of them. I switched to another top- ranked program that interested me without needing to experience the stressful transfer to another college or becoming unhappy in my current or another program.

Another planning consideration is the individual attention you might receive. Sometimes smaller or private colleges allow more personal attention, such as the willingness of professors to spend significant time with you or allow informal accommodations. In smaller classes you might have more opportunity to make comments or ask questions. Some large colleges or programs offer lectures in which students listen to a planned talk by an instructor with little to no interruption. While in those cases they might also offer smaller discussion sections, remembering what you might have wanted to say about the lecture might be more difficult, and the smaller section might be taught by a different instructor (such as a teaching assistant) who might give you a less precise answer. Then again, when I enjoyed a topic and a professor's teaching style, my favorite academic moments as an undergraduate came in the large lectures. Lectures offer a good opportunity to type notes on a laptop, and although classes with more active participation might make using a laptop less convenient, you might consider bringing one to all of your classes unless the instructor does not allow them.

Similarly, colleges differ in the disability accommodations and services they provide. Many colleges have more knowledge about how to accommodate students with physical or learning disabilities but lack effective resources for autistic people. They differ in the amount of, usefulness of, and process for obtaining accommodations. Colleges cannot modify content, require you to advocate for yourself, and may have stricter requirements for documenting your disability or challenges than in high school. I suggest you visit the student disability office before making your choice about colleges or at least before the school year begins if you can, to learn about what they offer and possibly register with them.

My personal experience provides some examples of how a disability office might help you, and also how that support differs across colleges. I have found that whereas I hardly ever used accommodations in middle school or high school, extended time on exams helped me greatly in college because of their less structured nature (such as fairly open-ended essays rather than choosing among specific answers). I also went through the disability office to get an accommodation to live in a single room on campus, which allowed me access to activities but also time alone for social or sensory reasons. I had to apply for whatever particular accommodations I believed I needed, whereas in graduate school at a different university, the disability office more proactively suggests accommodations for me (even those that I did not find helpful, such as note-taking). Few colleges offer personal help with time management to autistic students; if a college would offer you that accommodation, I think that might suggest its effectiveness in other areas.

Other issues to consider relate less to academics but still may matter greatly to you. The costs of attending college affect the decision of many college students, which includes thinking about how much your family will pay (if anything), how much and what types of financial support the college offers (such as scholarships or grants, loans, and Work-Study to earn money while in college), and how much money you would agree to pay back after graduation (if anything). This means, for example, that a private college that generally has much more expensive tuition and fees may become affordable if it offers you a huge scholarship, so I suggest you keep an open mind about your options but think critically when you must make a decision. You might consider the location of the program, such as proximity to family, your familiarity with or feelings toward the surrounding community, and the weather. Other factors that helped me to decide included extracurricular activities like student organizations, volunteering for community service, and cultural and athletic events.

Regardless of the college you choose, you will have various resources to help you address your needs. Each college has many offices or programs that serve students, and I suggest that you record the phone number of the ones most relevant to you and the college operator to direct you to others.

You might buy a planner or use organizers on your phone, if applicable. Also, you might carry a map of the campus, at least as you adjust. You can meet with instructors or contact them outside class, such as by e-mail. You might also see whether your program or college makes student evaluations of instructors available so you can choose one that best suits you. You also can try to get the contact information of at least one student in each class in case you need to ask about schoolwork, besides for possibly building social relationships with your peers.

Eventually you might think about transitioning to graduate school, the next level of higher education. Graduate school requires more independence and may have even less structure than college, and may value the research projects you do over grades. Many students have more active social lives as undergraduate college students than in graduate school, and you might find fewer opportunities for and less value in living on campus and participating actively in campus events in graduate school than earlier in college.

Despite these challenges, autistic people often have specific interests that graduate school allows us to specialize in to develop into more powerful talents, as well as other useful strengths such as logical or critical thinking skills. Too often non-autistic people misunderstand us and do not allow us the opportunities we need to succeed, but having an advanced degree might offer you more protection. Having more education may increase your chances of not only getting and keeping a job, but one in an area that interests you, with higher pay, and more freedom.

Self Accommodation

Leah Jane Grantham

In many ways, those of us who were born during the late '80s and beyond are among the luckiest, in terms of accommodation and disability services. In a pre-Americans With Disabilities Act world, getting even the most basic essentials to facilitate a successful and positive experience in work and life was a constant battle, with very few people who possessed the knowledge and passion to help you available.

Thanks to the passing of the ADA, much of that has been shifted in a more positive direction. When you first go to college, you will find that students with disabilities are now given legal protection and the opportunity to seek out the sources necessary to make college work for them. But we are not yet living in a post-ADA country. There are still many barriers that a student needs to overcome.

Sometimes, these things require a special knowledge on a particular topic, so you may turn to others to help you get what you need.

Other times though, you don't necessarily need a specialized skill set to accomplish getting what you need. In most situations, while a friend and advocate can be an invaluable source, all you really need is to look to yourself to get what is necessary.

Barriers take all sorts of forms at universities. Since autism is an invisible disability, it's not as easy to make clear what you need in order to function properly, compared to a student with a physical disability which is self- evident. Some people, such as professors, administrators, and university staff may express doubt about the existence of your disability. When I came to university, I had a difficult time with some people I was working with, who doubted that I had the same disability as "those kids on TV". This made for a hostile working environment, because I was unable to convincingly convey my need to have certain adjustments made for me to be at my top productivity as a student and work-study.

Such experiences can negatively color your experience with university, and may alienate you from accomplishing all that you can. It's very easy to get downhearted after requesting that the lights be turned down, or that earplugs be provided, and having people reject this request and doubting the validity of your disability. After my first encounter with such cynicism and outright disdain, I had a difficult time asking for anything, either from my disability coordinators, my professors, or people around me. I entered a state of passively attempting to make do with a series of irritating sensory overloads and hide my pain from the public eye.

Far from fixing the difficulties though, it caused my grades to downward spiral, and my personal life to suffer. I stopped enjoying activities that previously brought pleasure to me, and instead focused all of my time and energy on maintaining this false persona. It took a considerable amount of energy to keep it airtight in public, and in private, I had to resort to near constant stimming, to clear my brain of the overload de jour.

When I began to involve myself in disability advocacy projects though, I surrounded myself with a new type of people who changed the way I viewed asking for accommodation. When I first entered the room where we were meeting, I was asked, "Is there anything we can do to make you more comfortable?" It so happened that the room we were meeting in had a blackboard in it. I have a sensory issue with the sound, feeling, and look of chalk dust and chalk, making it extremely difficult for me to concentrate, when all I could focus on was desperately wanting to take a wet washrag and a bucket of warm, soapy water to clean off the blackboard.

I didn't make this evident until the end of the meeting, after deciding that it was worth taking the chance at being obnoxious to others in order to get away from the awful chalk. To my surprise, when I asked to have the meetings moved to a room where I didn't have to face a blackboard, I was met with a warm understanding and agreement to move. Sometimes, that's all it takes. I noticed that, once the relocation had taken place, I was able to fully participate in the board meeting, and became a very productive and popular member. Noticing the difference made me realize that, although certain people treated my requests for certain accommodations like a nuisance or a great struggle, they're not looking at the big picture. What these accommodations truly are is a vehicle for me so that I can equally participate in life. There may be barriers in their attitudes, but I resolved that I was going to push for my right to equal participation. That great epiphany helped me work with my disabilities coordinator behind the scene for certain accommodations (Scheduling tests in a private room, for instance) but I could depend upon myself in order to request other accommodations, or simply blaze my own path towards full participation.

Now, when I enter a classroom, I am fully equipped. I have earplugs in my pocket, and I have rehearsed simple phrases to explain their use. "I have sensory-processing disorder, this is in case I need to cope with unexpected sources of noise." I have special pouches filled with pleasant-feeling material, such as silk, so  that I can reach into the pouch to feel them when I need to feel something calming and soothing.

Part of self-accommodation was learning how to express my need for special considerations to all who may need to know. The other half was learning to take the initiative and proving just how necessary they were for me as a student and employee who wishes to exceed expectations and do the very best job possible.

Some special accommodations you use may strike those unfamiliar with their purpose as unusual, superfluous, or disruptive. You may elect to explain their purpose, but you can always remember that they are what works for you. You do not need to apologize for what makes you happy, and what is highest priority to you should be your right to participate equally in a classroom or workplace environment.

It's not easy to advocate for yourself, particularly if you prefer to communicate and express yourself in ways that are nonverbal, or are uncomfortable with verbal communication. I have issues with making my speech clear and understandable when in a tense or stressful situation, so I have found it helpful to not only practice what I want to say when explaining my accommodations, I also write it down and keep cards explaining the purpose of my tools and particular needs.

At the end of the day, you won't change everybody's mind. There will always be people who don't consider the benefits and joys of a diverse environment where people of various neurotypes are given the chance to participate on the same level as those who don't need to think twice about such things. It's okay if you fail to make them reconsider their previous prejudices. What matters most is making sure you have the chance to at least prove to yourself how your accommodations help you, no matter what they say. Be proud to fight for your right to be included.

Self Accommodation

Samantha April Davis

Accessible policy can make the difference between success in college and struggling against a system that does not accommodate your needs. Unfortunately, accessible policy is often not by default and must be secured through bureaucratic means. Furthermore, these bureaucracies are often ill suited to the needs of their clients or otherwise not accessible to those in need. When this is the case one must self-advocate for what they need.

One option when faced with an inaccessible institution is to work within the bureaucracy to try and work it to your advantage. This is not always easy, or possible, but has the advantage of being enforceable and consistent between classes and years.

A few tactics that may prove helpful in dealing with the accommodations process:

- If you have a mental health professional with whom you are working they should be the first person you discuss your academic needs with. Always discuss your needs, in detail, with this person as their report will serve as the guidelines the disability office will use in designing your accommodations. A few small changes to what your doctor writes—based on what you communicate to your doctor about your needs—can radically change the way accommodation negotiations play out later.

- A very common problem among autistic college students is that we lack official documentation for our autism or our documentation is out-of-date. Getting new documentation may not be practical or possible for whatever reason. Often in these circumstances the disability office wants to help you but is legally disallowed from providing assistance. Consider applying to the disability office under a related condition, such as anxiety, and working with your advisor to produce documentation that supports your needs. The disability office will likely be able to help you get a diagnosis or otherwise secure documentation you will need to do this.

- Consider seeking medical documentation for the most difficult parts of your autism, such as anxiety or learning difficulties. A mental health professional may be able to make a diagnosis or otherwise produce the salient paperwork without an autism diagnosis which could then be used to support each individual challenge one at a time. This may also be helpful when you have an autism diagnosis but the disability office refuses to recognize a specific aspect of your disability.

- Another way of handling the lack of documentation is to get your condition documented as a condition contributing to another, otherwise unrelated, condition. This is especially easy when working with psychologists and psychiatrists as all diagnoses made via the DSM-IV include other conditions the client has which contribute to the presentation of whatever disorder is being diagnosed. When part of a DSM-IV diagnosis these conditions are known as Axis-IV conditions. As an example, I am diagnosed with Tourette Syndrome and part of my diagnosis is the back pain that can be made worse by my tics.

When I sought official accommodations for my Tourette's I was offered accessible furniture for my back pain.

- Which advisor you have in the disability office can make a huge difference. You may be able to select which staff member you have. There is likely at least one disabled students' organization or club on campus. Try to get into contact with them and see what staff other autistic students have had success or trouble with. Listen to all the students there and try to select a staff member who has a reputation for being flexible, creative, and open-minded. This also applies to university psychologists and psychiatrists as their cooperation may be essential in providing solid support.

- The relationship between the client and the advisor is very important. This relationship, because of the personalities of both parties, may not develop as it should with every advisor. This is okay but it is important that you find an advisor who works well with you. If it is not, ask to see another that might provide a better fit for you. Advisors should understand this. This is especially important with your mental healthcare provider.

Another option for dealing with an inaccessible problem is to negotiate access directly with your professors and faculty. This has the advantage of being much more flexible in the face of unforeseen barriers as well as the advantage of not needing as much, if any, documentation. Of course, at the same time it suffers the disadvantage of relying on the good graces of your faculty. Nonetheless, because of the inflexibility of the bureaucratic system, even students with excellent accommodations through their disability office may have to resort to this from time to time. For many this may prove the only option available.

Some techniques for successfully negotiating with professors:

- Do your best to select good professors. When selecting your classes, ask others about various faculty members. This becomes more difficult when you are outside of your major but if your major has an academic club, association, lounge or other social space try to ask what other students think of various professors and who they would recommend for certain classes. A professor who has a good reputation as a teacher and who is invested and engaged with the success of their students is much more likely to take steps to ensure that a disabled or struggling student has the tools to succeed in their class. Select a professor based on how well they are known to work with students or how engaged they are in their teaching rather than on how easy they are.

- Start discussing your needs and difficulties with a professor early on in the semester, preferably within the first two weeks and preferably during their office hours or when other students are not distracting them. This is important because if the professor reacts with hostility it gives you the opportunity to change classes before the last day to drop or add classes has passed.

- If you can withstand the workload consider taking an extra class above-and-beyond what is required for being a full-time student or beyond what is required for financial assistance, if applicable. With the surplus units you have the ability to drop a hostile class without endangering your standing in college.

- Many of the things that pose barriers to your accessibility as an autistic individual may also prove familiar to a neurotypical person. For this reason it is not always necessary to frame your needs in relation to autism. A need may, in fact, be more relatable to a professor when framed simply as a need or an individual difficulty for you. Most professors are happy to provide support to a student who is struggling simply because they want you to succeed. It is possible for a professor to know you are autistic and for you to frame accessibility needs as personal requirements unrelated to your autism.

- The most important factor in having a positive experience with a professor is the professor understanding that you are invested in their class. The best way to do this is to regularly visit your professor with questions and comments after class or during their office hours. Interaction can be brief and can consist of a simple personal insight to how you relate to the material or what you think of it or a question. The important thing is that you consistently engage somehow with the professor face-to-face.

- Consider making an appointment with a professor to talk about your learning difficulties the week before semester starts. Very few students do this and it will allow you to start the semester in good standing. Even if you are unable to make such an appointment, the fact that you contacted them in order to do so will make you stand out. Be sure to introduce yourself as the person who asked for the appointment once you meet the professor.

- Interactions with the professor do not have to be culturally normative. For example, if you have social phobia consider writing comments or questions down on a pad of paper and showing it to the professor after class or during their office hours so you do not have to speak to them.

- Most departments have some kind of student club or organization affiliated with them. Other departments have student lounges. Consider participating in these organizations that are part of your major or minor. This will bring you into contact with other students who can help you in many ways. Participation in the student community of your department will also bring you into contact with your potential future faculty.

- Be prepared to negotiate. You may not always get the accommodations you desire. Rarely, however, will a member of the faculty leave a student with nothing. Negotiate, be honest with your needs and the difficulties you face, and establish a plan which both you and your professor feel is acceptable.

- Finally, communicate early and regularly. Approach the professor at the beginning of the semester to talk about access and continue this conversation. If you need to do so every week in order to work it into your routine, do so: Three minutes to say everything is alright this week can help when you need to say something is wrong.

Never be afraid to admit that you are struggling.

Never be afraid of admitting you need help and accommodations. It may not seem it at times when you are having difficulty but the faculty and staff want you to succeed. Even while they may not do the best job of accommodating your needs they are there to help you. At the very least, communicating your needs and difficulties lets the faculty understand that you care about your education and what they are teaching you.

Sensory Regulation

Alexander Eveleth

Like any public environment, going to college will expose you to a lot of unexpected and uncontrolled factors. Dining halls are one example—they tend to be full of people who don't share your sensory-regulation quirks, and who don't mind constant input from every direction. Your dorm-mates may like to play loud music during the daytime. And most dorms don't enforce quiet hours until times when people are traditionally sleeping. Worse still, from your perspective, you may find yourself at a dance party— something of the perfect storm for people who process sensory input in an abnormal way. Parties are loud. A lot of college students have no ill effects, neurologically at least, from music played at levels that might leave them deaf in their old age. Parties are frequently full of inputs of all types from all directions—smells, music and raised voices, flashing lights, smoke machines, etc.—that can interact negatively with the parts of your brain that process the information gathered by your senses.

The key to coexisting with people who don't share your neurological differences is to remain calm. If the dining hall is too much for you, find an alternative place to eat your meals, figure out when it is less crowded, or go shopping and start packing meals for yourself. If a dorm-mate plays their music too loudly, politely request that they turn it down. You don't need to identify that the issue comes from your neurological status—you only need to express your preference. Most people will do the polite thing and try not to bother you. And if parties are too much for you, find a level of sensory input that works for you. That may include not going at all, sticking mostly to the outside (the fringes of dance parties are social gathering points for people who want to hear each other talk), or taking breaks from the stimulation. You may find yourself acclimating with time—personally, I found that the duration of time I could stand to be on a noisy dance floor increased through my time spent at college. If that happens, cool. If it doesn't, don't sweat it. If you don't make a big deal out of it, nobody will really notice.

That's important to remember: if you take the initiative, and manage your senses, nobody will think anything out of the ordinary is going on, so if you're worried about people seeing you having sensory trouble, remember not to overestimate their attentiveness.

If you're living in the dorms, there's a line to be walked between sensory peace and getting along with your neighbors. Your school may have a "quiet dorm" option that gives you a place to live with fewer interruptions. But even there, you might have problems. You shouldn't have to put up with sensory regulation issues in your living space, but you still need to live with your neighbors. If someone is causing a problem, the first step is addressing the issue politely. See if whoever is causing a problem, let's say with music, will fix it (loud music is one of the most common problems between dorm-mates, even in the absence of sensory regulation matters).

If the problem persists—let's say they decline your request to turn down the music—the college will have provided you with means to resolve the issue. You can talk to your Resident Assistant (RA) or equivalent about it— it's their job to resolve conflicts over personal comfort. You have a right to your own comfort at reasonable hours, though the RA or your dorm in general might have defined quiet and non-quiet hours.

Sound probably won't be your only problem. Areas of your campus will be hotspots for smokers of various things—if it bothers you, avoid them.

As a general rule, if you find yourself becoming overwhelmed, leave the area that's bothering you until you feel better—your health and comfort is more important than whatever brought you there, guaranteed. Take the time to take care of yourself. The party will be there when you get back.

Better Living through Prosthetic Brain Parts

Zoe Gross

Hi! I'm Zoe, I'm an autistic college student, and I'm learning to manage my life. In high school, my parents helped me stay organized. If I forgot to eat dinner, they would remind me, and if I was behind schedule they would hurry me up. At college, I am the one arranging my schedule, forcing myself to do schoolwork, and reminding myself to eat dinner. If I forget about an appointment, no one will remember it for me. If I go back to sleep after my alarm clock goes off, no one can save me from missing class.

For a lot of college students, this freedom is a purely good thing, but for me it comes with a cost. Because of the way my disability affects me, I don't already have the structures in my brain that my classmates are using to keep themselves organized. I'm still working on my strategies for dealing with this. So far, I've discovered some tools that I use to keep me on track. I call these tools "prosthetic brain parts" because they prop up the parts of my brain that don't always work as well as I would like. While the specific things I use might not work for you, hopefully this list will give you some good ideas.

VISUAL TIMER

Brain function boosted: Relationship to Time

If you're like me and have trouble conceptualizing time, a visual timer might help you. On a timer like the one pictured here, the red area slowly decreases as time passes, showing you how much time has elapsed and how much you have left. They come in a lot of sizes, so they're fairly portable. You can set some types of visual timers to beep when the time is up.

There are lots of ways to use a timer to help you live independently. I set mine to show the amount of time left before I leave for class in the morning, and that helps me pace myself while I'm getting dressed and packing my books. These are also good for transitioning between activities. For example, if I'm watching YouTube videos but will have to switch to homework soon, I might set the timer for ten more minutes, and glance at it occasionally to see how much time I have left before I change activities. This makes the transition much less abrupt.

You can also use timers for doing homework. Set it for an hour, and then work until it winds down. Set it for half an hour, and then take a break until it winds down. Repeat. If you're going to try this, I'd encourage you to vary

the length of your study periods and break periods until you find what works best for you. Some people can work uninterrupted for two hours and then need longer breaks. Other people can only focus for half an hour at a time and might take shorter breaks.

CALENDARS AND PLANNERS

Brain function boosted: Long- and Short-Term Planning

At college, you will have a lot of dates and deadlines to manage – not just schoolwork due dates, but paperwork such as housing and financial aid forms as well. It helps to have a calendar so that you can record and remember these due dates, and take a long-term overview of the tasks you have to complete each semester.

Just as you can schedule a semester with a calendar, you can schedule a day with a planner, which breaks every day into hour or half-hour slots. Filling in a planner allows you to see visually how much time you are devoting to

each activity. If you find color-coding helpful, you can use one color for scheduling studying, another color for appointments, and so on.

For some people, a three-dimensional paper calendar or planner works best, but other people find it helps to keep a virtual calendar on their computer. If you spend a large portion of your day on the computer, I recommend keeping your calendar there. You can use a program with a calendar component, such as Outlook, or set up a Google Calendar for free.

If you have a Smartphone, you can keep your calendar and planner there. This makes it easier to check and update your calendar wherever you are.

LISTS AND FLOW CHARTS

Brain function boosted: Task Analysis

One of the first problems I encountered at college was getting out of my room in the mornings. There are so many small steps between waking up and walking out the door (getting up, showering, dressing, packing...). I don't think very fast first thing in the morning, so keeping these steps straight became a real challenge.

I actually have this problem with a lot of things that are broken down into small steps, including academic tasks like writing essays. Something recently learned, and found very helpful, was that these complex, multi-step tasks can be written up as flow charts or numbered lists. For me, making a flow chart that explains the process of leaving my room in the

morning makes that process concrete, and I can refer to the chart if I forget what I'm doing while getting dressed.

I make my flow charts by hand, but if this doesn't appeal to you, there are websites online where you can make flow charts from templates.

ALARMS AND WAKE-UP CALLS

Brain function boosted: Super-Ego

Getting a good night's sleep is important for college students, but sometimes a heavy workload or a night out with friends means you have to make do with less than eight hours. But you still have to get up and go to class the next day, which means you have to wake up when your alarm clock goes off. I have a lot of trouble with this – I have often woken up late, having missed a class, with no memory of turning the alarm clock off and going back to sleep.

The trick of waking up in the morning is to keep yourself awake long enough for your sense of responsibility to kick in. At that point, you'll remember why it's important to get up and go to class. There are several ways of achieving this – setting several alarms, or purchasing one of those fancy alarm clocks which runs away from you on wheels, forcing you to chase it around the room. Alternately, you can try signing up at a website such as snoozester.com, which will send you automated wake-up calls until you press the right button to indicate that you are awake.

OTHER PEOPLE

Brain function boosted: Any of the Above

Even though you're at college and you're becoming more independent, there will still be times when you need help from other people, and that's okay. Check to see what services your college provides for students with disabilities. It's possible that you might be able to find a tutor or coach to help you with academics and organization.

If you find friends who are willing to call you and wake up in the morning, or help you focus while you study, there's nothing wrong with asking them for help. While you might have more trouble with organization than most people, remember that your classmates are also living on their own for the first time, and they may be facing some of the same issues. If you sometimes need someone else's help in order to focus on your schoolwork, try studying with a friend. It could turn out that you distract each other – or you could end up helping to keep each other on task.

I hope these tips helped you as much as they've helped me. Please remember that there will be times when you forget assignments or sleep through classes, and that doesn't make you a bad person – it's part of adjusting to life in a new environment. Developing your coping strategies is a gradual process, and sometimes it can be stressful. But once you find the tools that work for you, they will continue to help you long after college is

Autism and Dorm Life

Lydia Brown

Sometime back in late May or early June, I submitted a medical request for special housing to the Academic Resource Center. My request was filed on the basis of Asperger's Syndrome and Sensory Processing Disorder, and requested a single room (as opposed to having one or more roommates) in order to best accommodate me and prevent unfortunate situations. I learned the other day that my request was approved, so I will be living in a single dorm this year.

But why might a single room be a good idea for the Autistic college student? There are several reasons.

I have heard several horror stories from other Autistic college students or recent graduates who had horrible experiences with the complex social issues of living with a roommate and who ultimately found reprieve in a single room as upperclassmen. Being friends or even friendly with a person is vastly different than having to live in the same small room with him or her. If you are co- habiting, you have to make decisions about who is allowed to do what and who is responsible for doing what, as well as what is forbidden or restricted. If there are problems, you are adults and you are responsible for attempting to resolve the problem on your own before seeking outside aid, such as from an R.A. or someone in the Office of Housing. These are not the kinds of social situations usually discussed or addressed in most social skills classes, nor encountered anywhere but college (or, perhaps, the military.) They are more complex and intricate than determining whether a relationship with another person is friendly or trustworthy, or potentially harmful or disadvantageous. You are forced to interact with this person on many levels, and for the Autistic person, that can be overwhelming, daunting, and exceedingly difficult, especially if the roommate happens to be a neurotypical.

Then you have the sensory concerns. First of all, most of us find that we need time to be alone, to rest and recover from overstimulation—sensory, social, or otherwise—that has accumulated throughout a day, and to recharge for the next day or the next event to which we must subject ourselves. That kind of solace and isolation is often found in a private space such as a bedroom. But if you are living in a space where you have a roommate, there is no guarantee that you will have any such alone time to recover. In fact, because your roommate *also* lives in the same room, he or she has an equal right to be there at any or all times, and you have absolutely no right, ever, at any time to ask or force your roommate to leave except by mutual consent (which again, cannot be guaranteed.) You will then be trapped in a vicious cycle of constant social interaction and stimulation, and little opportunity to recover from it.

Remember, it's not that Autistic people are inherently anti-social or hate other people. Instead, social interactions are much harder for us, more enervating, and far more costly; thus, we need this time alone in order to be able to socialize with you.

But back to sensory concerns. Other than the need to recover from social and sensory overstimulation throughout the day, there are also concerns of sensory stimuli in the room itself. What if the roommate likes to wear cologne or perfume, or use other scented hygienic products, or use a room freshener? What if the roommate likes to play his or her music too loudly or too softly, or puts his or her possessions in bizarre orders? You can't force your roommate to change anything about the way he or she acts. You can ask nicely for him or her to reasonably accommodate you, and you can hope, during the roommate matching process, that your roommate won't be someone who would do things that would irritate certain sensory sensibilities.

In fact, Georgetown has a unique roommate matching system called Charms, that acts much like a dating service but for roommate matching. Ostensibly, students complete an anonymous profile including preferences like bedtime, temperature, cleanliness, willingness to share belongings, and frequency of visitors to the dorm, and can then search for other same-sex students with similar profiles. Upon seeing people with matching responses, students can initiative anonymous messaging with their matches. If they like one another enough through the additional questioning, they can both request to be each other's roommate, and will be paired together if and only if they request each other.

While waiting for my request to be processed and either granted or denied, I was instructed to complete this form in the event it was denied (and that the Academic Resource Center would override this assignment were my request granted), and so I did. In the last part of the profile, under additional information, I was sure to include a stipulation that anyone living with me would have to agree not to use any scented hygienic products or cleaning chemicals in our room at any time. (I did get one response before I was able to withdraw my profile from the Charms process.) But even were I to have been matched with a person who would have agreed to that request (perhaps someone who was allergic to scented to products), there are any number of other sensory issues that I could not have possibly covered in such a brief profile or even in conversations. Some may not be addressed until they become a problem, and it would be better not to create that problem if it can be avoided without any significant cost.

So what does having a single room mean? For one, it doesn't mean that I will necessarily be isolated from social life or activities on my floor. I will be part of a Living and Learning Community (see application essay below), which will have planned activities every so often, and which occupies my entire floor. It does mean that I will have the option of spending time alone to recover from social interaction after spending a day socializing. It means I can choose to be involved in informal or formal activities. I can always invite other girls to visit me in my dorm, too, at my initiative.

It means that I have taken an important step in securing for myself a necessary accommodation to promote my own emotional and social health. After all, it is important for any person, student or not, Autistic or not, to be happy and healthy in all possible ways. In my case, and for many Autistic college students, a single room may be the best option for the flexibility and freedom it gives us.

Independent Campus Living

Alexander Eveleth

It's possible that college will represent the first time you've had to live independently and take charge of taking care of yourself. Don't worry about that if it's the case. There are plenty of people like you living independently around the world.

Independent living represents a new set of challenges for everybody, and not just you. You'll be far from the only person arriving on campus having little experience managing all the aspects of your own life.

It will probably help to plan a schedule around classes and schoolwork (for example, if you have a break between two classes, consider going to the library to get some reading done). You may find it beneficial to plan your day out in more detail than others might, in order to help you to manage class-time, assigned work, and essentials such as eating, grooming, etc.

One of my friends is making a difficult class schedule work this semester by scheduling every part of the day. If it helps you get things done, go ahead and plan things such as your study time. For example, it might help to have a notebook in which you document your obligations or interests such as assigned work, evening events, and meetings with your professors. I started keeping a notebook with weekly to-do lists during freshman year and have continued the practice thus far. Remember that maintenance of the essentials will help you keep going on academics—you won't be as effective in the library if you're missing sleep, meals, or showers.

You'll hopefully learn when to balance the tasks of academics and taking care of yourself. The college student strung out on a constant barrage of caffeine to fuel all-nighters, unkempt and unshaven, might be a common image when we think about colleges, especially academically rigorous ones, but it doesn't have to be you. If you manage things correctly, the times when you need to pull all-nighters—and there will be times like that, almost certainly—can find you showered, shaved, and ready.

There's a lot of science out there to tell you that your mental performance is dependent on being well fed and rested, but another important factor is feeling good. If you feel gross because you haven't showered, you won't perform well in class or on tests. Get your work done, but take care of yourself while you're at it. Don't let yourself get so stressed that it hurts your ability to do work.

Autism & Independent Living in College

Leah Jane Grantham

I frequently heard this old expression from the parents of my friends when we were teenagers: "Eighteen and you're out the door!" My mother said that in so many words to me, but I did end up leaving my home at seventeen, a few weeks shy of my eighteenth birthday. I had purposefully picked a university far from my home, so that I would be forced to learn to get along with people outside of my family. It wasn't always so successful, but I learned a considerable amount along the way about personal space, the meaning of friendship, and overcoming the awkwardness of undressing in front of someone who's not connected to you by blood or romance. So far in my college career I have lived with five roommates. The first four were in a dormitory setting, so we had a reduced degree of privacy and personal space to work with.

But, while living in the dormitories, I had the advantage of being assigned to one of the quieter buildings on campus, a single-sex dormitory for women. That in and of itself has its own set of perks and drawbacks. It also proved to be quieter and less triggering, sensory-processing wise. If at all possible, I would recommend talking with the campus housing representatives or office to explain why it is a high priority that you get a relatively quiet and peaceful dormitory. The disability services or perhaps a high school counselor can assist with this. You're usually given the chance to fill out your preference when filling out a housing application, but when a school has high enrollment numbers, it may be a good idea to not leave it up to fate. The more quiet and studying-oriented dormitories tend to fill up quickly, disability services and early enrollment are key. If you are uncomfortable with speaking to them, a letter or email explaining your situation will suffice. You can ask a trusted friend or advocate to write it for you if you are unsure as to how to articulate your request.

It never occurred to me to ask for a single-person bedroom, though it would have been within my right to do so as a disabled student. My primary discouragement from asking was the fact that the private rooms tended to be placed on the bottom/basement level of every dormitory, with windows almost deviously placed at the level of the parking lot. Cars would go in and out and spew their exhaust into the rooms, choking any unfortunate residents. Between a desire for privacy and wanting to keep the possibility of contracting asthma and other lung conditions to a minimum, the former lost out. Besides, I had promised myself that I would try my best to get along with other people in college, not only for myself, but also for the sake of my mother. It was her highest wish for me to learn how to be independent, and I wanted to make her proud.

My experience with living with roommates in the dormitories has had its own set of advantages and difficulties. The biggest disadvantage which springs to memory is the fact that my roommates had a penchant for bringing friends (and in some case, boyfriends) home with them to chat, or have a sleepover, or watch a movie. In such a confined space, the noise of conversation and activities would disturb me from my homework and my sleep. At the time, I was unsure how to deal with it. I was too frightened to confront my roommates, even though they were cordial people, I simply have a strong dislike of confrontation. Ultimately, if I could go back in time, I would either give a letter to the Residence Assistance (RA) of my floor, or else write a letter to my roommates, asking a few of them to please find a neutral third-party spot to meet while I was sleeping or studying. It is after all, a university policy that your right to sleep and study outweighs the right of anyone else to socialize.

There were some definite perks to make the lack of privacy a bit less problematic, in the long run. I have difficulties falling and staying asleep, and sometimes I can have erratic hours of sleep, and it proved to be a significant preventative measure against tardiness to live right on campus. I could roll out of bed 20 minutes before my first class and still manage to get there on time, a luxury I lost upon moving into the off-campus apartments. There was also the advantage of the meal plan, which, for someone like me, whose cooking skills are spotty, made nutrition and maintaining a regular schedule of eating easier. Since fresh vegetables and fruits are expensive and can be time-consuming to prepare in a tasty fashion, being a 5-minute walk to the "Food Zoo" to pick out a salad and soup was a luxury I still miss sometimes!

Privacy for stimming and other activities became a rare and in between luxury in the dorms, sadly. Even with overly social roommates who were frequently out with friends, they would return unexpectedly, and I was too embarrassed and self-conscious to stim in front of someone who wasn't family. I was further deterred from stimming by the lack of comfortable furniture in the dormitory; the furniture provided consisted of a desk and hard back chair and the bed. Some dorms may provide couches which are more welcoming to stimming, but mine was not, and the bed was too high to stim without fear of falling out and breaking something.

Unfortunately, good, plushy furniture tends to be expensive. The single- best solution for lack of comfortable stimming furniture though, is wonderfully cheap. I acquired a lovely beanbag chair, and after that, I could stim peacefully when I was in private. They can be found on a sliding scale of cheapness at most big-box stores, and if the tactile sensation is to your liking, they are a lifesaver for when you have limited furniture. When it comes to privacy for stimming, if you are in a dormitory that has no privacy, try either staking out a private space outside of your dorm room, wherever you feel most comfortable, or try to learn the habits and schedule of your roommate, explaining to them that you need x O'clock to Y O'clock on Z day as a private time, and see if they agree to find an activity outside of the dorm to do. Most people will be amicable about this if you make it clear from the beginning that you just need this alone time.

Conversely, I wholeheartedly recommend spending as little time in your dorm room as possible. It may be a safe space and wonderful to return to in order to calm yourself down and find your ground, but there is freedom and joy in just wandering around the town or campus. If you are new to the town, then this is especially important, as it will give you a sense of things. If you have a poor sense of direction and worry you couldn't find your way back, try going with a trusted friend. Or, if you wish to have alone time, a service dog/animal is a wonderful way of getting around town without having to worry about being impeded by a poor sense of direction. If you are new to the town, both you and the service animal needs to get used to these new places, but after a while, it will be second nature to the dog to go to any place in town.

I found the local library to be a marvelous sanctuary for when I needed to get away from my dorm room. Like many people, I felt it necessary when I moved to Missoula to cultivate a "third space", that is, somewhere that was not school, work, or my dorm, where I could go to clear my head and enjoy myself. Coffee houses are popular in college areas, but be sure to bring earplugs if your ears are sensitive, they can be noisy. I personally adore the smell of coffee roasting and tea brewing, but the smells can be bothersome for those with sensitive nostrils. Whatever works for you as a sanctuary, seek it out. They can be the best part of living independently.

All in all, the best advice I can give when choosing to live independently is to consider what you want out of the experience, and try to make that a reality. You have every right to expect to be treated with courtesy and have your accommodations met by your university and potential landlords.

Don't be bullied or forced to believe that you will not be able to live independently without accepting that you can't have your accommodations. They are part of the set that will help you lead a happy, fulfilling independent life while in college.

Health and Wellness

Steven Kapp

Achieving a healthy lifestyle through an appropriate balance of diet, exercise, and sleep may become more difficult, but possibly more

important, in college. The less structured nature of college, including greater demands on time management and need for independence, can pose obstacles for anyone in maintaining a routine schedule. Many autistic people especially need and thrive on structure, but might have sleep issues like insomnia, or might be picky – and perhaps not the most health-conscious – eaters, and might not get regular physical activity. I have experienced challenges and some success in these areas, and consider them a foundation for taking care of one's health needs. They may reduce the need for formal help, but your campus's health and counseling centers and disability offices also may provide support.

Sleep

I found it much easier to sleep at a consistent and productive amount before college. Homework was usually assigned the same day as a relevant lesson and due the following day, so I took a break when I got home from school and generally worked until I completed all my assignments. School began and ended at the same time most days, so while I sometimes slept in on the weekend, my mind and body had become familiar with the schedule and would collect extra rest as needed. I also lived with my parents, who usually did not allow me to stay up late for homework, which added pressure for me to not procrastinate. In college, however, classes often begin at different times across the week and you may be expected to have more responsibility for your schedule even if you live with your parents (as is the case for me now in graduate school). Assignments tend to take place on a longer term, often several weeks or the course of the term.

Nevertheless, try to regulate sleep in college; I have found it to be one of the most important factors in my academic productivity and psychological well-being. I can easily feel depressed when I oversleep and anxious or depressed when sleep-deprived. Various autistic and non-autistic people alike have managed to pace themselves by scheduling their activities into time blocks (such as on their phone or a pocket calendar). I usually have tried to set realistic goals for what to accomplish that same day so that I have more flexibility and reduce the risk of sacrificing quality for time concerns. All this becomes easier if you have a regular flow of mental, emotional, and physical energy from sleeping well. Seek and use accommodations for extended time as needed, practice strategies that work for you, and make sure to have a relaxing bedtime routine and set your alarm to a reasonable time. I also recommend that if you live on or near campus that you have your own room or request a roommate who has compatible sleeping habits. I lived on campus for all four of my undergraduate years but only had a roommate for one semester because I woke up from the light or sound whenever he entered the room in the middle of the night. Therefore you may need sensory self-accommodations such as earphones or a sleep mask.

DIET

Also remember to drink and eat well. Many students consume caffeinated beverages or energy drinks, but should monitor their intake so they do not disrupt sleep, or cause or contribute to mood swings or medical concerns. A cup or two of coffee or similar caffeinated beverages a day is fine, and is better than extremes of drinking nothing to too much, which I have experienced. Unfortunately, because of anxiety, busyness, and not planning or making decisions well, I developed a bad habit in college of staying up extremely late to write an essay or study for an exam. This required a lot of caffeine, which made me more nervous and could take days to recover from (such as a strong headache). Many people also cannot perform well academically under those conditions.

Moreover, if you choose to drink alcohol, please do so safely (know what you are drinking, have a safe amount, do not drink and drive, and so on) and legally (at least age 21). You may find a non-alcoholic drink available, and if there is none or you face relentless peer pressure, you might consider removing yourself from the situation. Drinking to fit in may not be a smart idea, and for autistic people drinking may have the opposite effect.

Alcohol often reduces people's judgment, so after drinking your more natural, socially unusual behaviors may stand out more. Therefore, although many people drink to fit in, drinking might make you more likely to get socially rejected and ultimately feel more self-conscious.

Similarly, having a reasonably healthy or balanced diet can promote a stable, good mood and good physical health. I had an extremely limited diet when I arrived at college, but cafeteria-style campus dining offers such a variety of choices that I felt comfortable. Since it was all-you-can-eat, it allowed me a safe environment to try new foods. Having an unlimited meal plan that restricted me to the dining halls also allowed me to better pace my meals into more and smaller sittings for better metabolism, or a more even pace of energy. This dining choice requires self-discipline but allows diverse eaters healthy choices, and does not require the skills of making one's own food. Eating at restaurants, which may be on campus, may be convenient or tasty, but not as healthy. You might stop by or look online to check the menu, for both general nutrition and preparing in advance in case you go with others and wish to decide on your meal more quickly. Another choice is to bring food from home, which I have done in graduate school when the cafeterias have not been as accessible.

EXERCISE

My best period of mental and physical health during adolescence and young adulthood (so far) took place when, and largely because, I had a progressive exercise routine, so I highly recommend a physically active lifestyle that has some structure. I have always been clumsy and uncoordinated; growing up I was one of the last students to get chosen in physical education, and I had little physical activity outside of school. I had never worked out in a gym until college, but gyms have many options for a wide variety of interests and abilities. Many, if not most, colleges have a gym, and your tuition may entirely or at least mostly cover its price so exercising there might be an affordable habit. It also might be a convenient choice, especially for students who live on or near campus, and have a variety of hours that can work with your schedule. Nevertheless, it is a good idea to find out the hours of operation and when the parts of it of interest to you are less likely to be busy so you can plan accordingly.

Again, there are many options for working out. Cardiovascular exercise using treadmills and the elliptical, or simply walking or running, may leave a relaxing feeling and may lower blood pressure since it works the heart and lungs. Weight training equipment works the muscles and may improve strength and toning, but as with any exercise make sure that you do not overstrain yourself; it is safer, as I do and recommend, to use machines rather than free weights that require balance and good techniques.

Exercise in general may improve flexibility, coordination, energy and endurance, memory, attention, sleep, relaxation, metabolism, appearance, and weight. The body also might release hormones called endorphins that improve mood, which you may be able to feel during exercise and long afterward. For me and many others exercise has acted as a natural antidepressant, but it requires commitment – and increased intensity for better results – that many people struggle to maintain.

Try not to be too hard on yourself if you encounter challenges in establishing, continuing, or progressing an exercise regimen – I still have not created one in graduate school despite some success at times as an undergraduate – but you might have many choices for how to get active. Perhaps taking an optional physical education class (not necessarily for a grade – your choice) would help you learn how to exercise and help you keep a schedule. I took a weight training class, and without it I do not know if I would have had the courage to begin using related equipment. Many colleges offer group recreation classes (such as dance or yoga); they looked too overstimulating from a sensory and social standpoint to me, but you might find it a good opportunity to learn from an instructor, keep a routine (notice a theme?), and make a workout partner or friend. If you need additional help, your college might offer personal trainers that you might have to pay, an option I never tried; you could more likely find one at a private gym if interested too.

HYGIENE AND GROOMING

Despite the importance of sleep, diet, and exercise to health promotion, they may have a less direct social effect than cosmetic or superficial habits. While many people in general do not sleep, eat, and exercise well and such a healthy lifestyle requires extensive time and commitment, people might only give off indirect direct signs of these efforts (such as tiredness or their weight). Yet not taking a moment to brush one's hair might be more likely to affect others' impressions of you and possibly contribute to rejection; they might think that you do not take care of yourself so they assume that you will not respect them, when you simply forget or did not think that aspect of appearance mattered. Some activities like brushing teeth do directly impact health in important ways as well as social presentation (better-looking teeth and better-smelling breath). Other matters of hygiene, grooming, and other acts of self-care, however, relate only to making people comfortable or yourself look good, such as shaving regularly; putting on deodorant; and wearing clean, unwrinkled clothes that fit the context (such as level of formality).

THERAPY

Exercising flexibility and self-discipline in response to life's challenges are generally difficult skills, and you might seek professional help to cope and adapt in a way that works for you. I have focused mainly on what you can do to help yourself on your own or with unofficial assistance, because they reflect general lifestyle habits, some of which may be relatively available, convenient, or affordable. Formal options like therapy may also prove useful to you, and you may wish to think about them more carefully because they may vary more depending on your personal abilities and needs. Through the campus counseling center, disability office, or privately you can see an individual therapist. You may have limited options through your college, such as a small number of sessions or providers, but having therapy through your school might be convenient or less expensive (maybe even covered by tuition). Good therapists understand, respect, and communicate well with their clients with useful feedback. I do not think they need expertise in or experience working with autistic people, since they need to see you as an individual and you might think their ideas about the autism spectrum do not relate to you.

On the other hand, having a therapist with some background in autism or experience working with autistic people might help you since many autistic people may not benefit from common types of therapy. For example, people receiving psychotherapy often must build a personal relationship with their therapist based on somewhat free-flowing interactions about their emotions. If you have such a therapist, he or she might expect you to initiate or lead these dynamic conversations; you may wish to request a modification if possible and if you find this approach exhausting or confusing. Traditional psychodynamic therapists may relate some of your challenges to your family upbringing, which I have found emotionally difficult and not constructive, especially when I have lived with my parents and wish to maintain a respectful relationship with them.

Instead, other methods like cognitive-behavioral therapy and mindfulness- based stress reduction might offer more advantages to you. Cognitive- behavioral therapy might help teach you practical skills to make sense of your thoughts and emotions so you can function more independently, rather than focusing narrowly on feeling good in the short term or trying to become "normal". It offers logic and structure with which many autistic people thrive. As another option, mindfulness may help you attend to the moment and become more open-minded about and accepting of your thoughts, feelings, and sensations. This approach may particularly help self-regulation in autistic people who have ruminative or repetitive thoughts that cause distress, or who may find it helpful to cope with sensory overload. For example, I sometimes think more critically and analytically than I would like, and mindfulness might help soothe someone like me with a non-judgmental attitude, rather than actively attacking and facing irrational thoughts as cognitive-behavioral therapy encourages.

Your college might offer support groups in addition to individual therapy. The opportunity to make connections with similar others may improve self understanding through dialogue about others' experiences. You might form friendships with others you meet in the group, and ideally the group will help you develop skills to improve relationships with people in other contexts. Well-run groups do not tolerate pity or disrespect, although you may sense a negative tone from sessions, such as other people's stories, that might overwhelm you. If you become involved in therapy but it seems unhelpful, you might consider waiting before making a decision because progress may take time after a difficult beginning, but you reserve the right to end therapy.

MEDICATION

Psychotropic medication is an individual choice that some autistic people make to manage anxiety, depression, or other disabilities. Medications vary in their class (the types of actions they perform), and within each class in intensity, effectiveness, specific functions, or side effects. I recommend informing yourself about possible benefits and costs as much as possible, from doing your own "research" (for example, looking up information online, asking trusted people you know who have personal experience with related conditions or medications, and asking relevant professionals such as psychiatrists, other medical doctors, or pharmacists). All medications potentially carry side effects, so it is important to know about the range of effects they can have. Similarly, understand your right to refuse medication (except in some circumstances in which a medical professional declares you dangerous, which happens too often because of misunderstandings).

You also reserve the right to receive a lower dosage than, or to suggest a different medication from, what your doctor recommends. This may especially be helpful for autistic people, since many of us are particularly sensitive to medication, both in terms of needing smaller amounts to have effective results and having more or stronger side effects than many people at higher levels, and no medication has federal approval for specific use with autistic adults. This simply means that many doctors are not well educated about which medications may help autistic people, but it is possible that medications that have helped others with similar needs as you may benefit you as well. For example, some autistic people successfully use antidepressants like SSRIs to elevate their mood.

The timing of medication poses additional considerations. If you decide to begin or discontinue psychotropic medication in consultation with your doctor, it may help to do so at a relatively ordinary time rather than one of increased transition or stress in case you react sensitively, at least briefly, to the change. Depending on your circumstances and under professional supervision, you may choose to use multiple medications simultaneously (perhaps for different purposes), or medication in combination with psychotherapy or other tools or strategies to improve your mental health, and it may be wise to add or remove these different components separately so you can better identify the effect of each decision.

I hope you find these suggestions empowering. My mother pressured me to use medication to treat depression late in high school beginning before I became a legal adult, and a psychiatrist in graduate school pressured me to use a dose of a medication outside my comfort zone, so I hope the knowledge of your rights and responsibilities to make your own decisions will ensure that you have a better experience, whatever choices you make.

OTHER MEDICAL CARE

As an adult, you may undertake more responsibility about your general physical health and schedule your own medical appointments, such as undergoing the recommended annual physical examination. Again, attending to your health may be more convenient and possibly less expensive if done on campus. Many campuses have a health center and require students to carry health insurance. I suggest you compare the cost and benefits of your current health insurance plan and insurance your college offers, if applicable, and choose the plan that works best for you. I also recommend that you record the phone number and hours of the health center and know the procedures and resources available in case of an emergency.

Mental Health

Leah Jane Grantham

Mental health is a difficult issue for me to talk about. I hardly feel like an expert on the subject, since I continue to work towards resolving my own issues with mental health. However, compared to when I first began college, I feel I've developed a much stronger grasp on how to manage difficulties that may arise from mental health issues, and it is my hope that this can serve as a guide for those who also need to consider the challenges to mental health going to college can present.

Being a neuro-atypical college student is difficult to begin with. In my case, high school was a trying experience, after dealing with bullies, issues with anxiety, and a multitude of other issues. If I could go back in time, I would have considered the option of taking a year off of schooling altogether, to collect my thoughts and mentally prepare myself for the challenges of college.

Taking a year off is a luxury many people cannot consider, but if there is a possibility for you, after graduating from high school, obtaining a GED or equivalent, it's worth considering. The time can be spent either pursuing a hobby, contacting a local business to see if they offer part-time jobs in a field that interests you, or, if you feel prepared and have a passion for it, volunteering. When I was close to finishing high school, I had a job working at a horse stable. I had minimal contact with people, and could focus all of my energy on interacting with the animals, which proved to be great company. Looking back, I wish I had taken some more time to work at the stable. It proved to be the most helpful thing towards managing my troubles in high school, and functioned essentially as a form of therapy for me during a very difficult time. I can't imagine what a rewarding experience it would have been if I had been able to do my work at the ranch without having to deal with high school. It would have given me a "breather" in colloquial terms, allowing me time to rejuvenate in preparation for college.

Once I actually got to college, the greatest difficulties I faced were related to social issues. I had little difficulty interacting with my professors; I've always gotten along easier with adults than with people in my own age bracket. But my fellow classmates posed a challenge for me, the rules appeared to be much more intricate and dependent upon presumed mutually understood social mores than in high school. It also took on a new, subtler level of bullying which proved to be more psychologically devastating than what I had experienced in high school.

After a particularly nasty incident of being bullied and belittled by classmates, I suffered a panic attack, which left me on anti-anxiety medications. Even with the medication, I still suffered from panic attacks, to the point where I was fearful that I would have to seek a medical withdrawal from college. Nothing in my mind would have been more devastating than to admit defeat after working so hard to get accepted as a candidate for higher education. The medicine was the type that was to be taken upon the onset of the attack. It was up to me to find out what was causing them, and take preventative measures.

I decided it would be best if I sought the university's health center for advice on how to protect myself from these attacks. They had a counseling and psychological services, but none of the counselors had any experience treating an autistic patient. Faced with a Sophie's choice of either getting no treatment at all, or going to a cost-prohibitive specialist located outside the city limits, I vowed I would be the one to educate my therapist. In my case, this turned out to be the best option. My therapist was open minded, kind, and more than willing to listen to my side of the story. I feel like she looked forward to our Tuesday appointments as much as I did.

Sometimes though, choosing this method can backfire. After similar issues with mental health, my partner, also autistic, decided to use the university's counseling program. However, at my partner's university, there was a "peer counseling" program instead of one with bona fide counselors. The counseling student assigned to my partner was dismissive of the idea that autism existed in adults, voicing the opinion that autism was mainly concocted by pharmaceutical companies to hock pills at an unsuspecting public. Needless to say, my partner was forced to seek a private practice to deal with mental health issues. It's a gamble, but if you find you have a good rapport with a counselor, or if they are familiar with autism and display a willingness to listen to you, it's worth considering talking with them.

Sadly, my classmates were not the only source of bullying I encountered. Unfortunately, professors, bosses, and administrators are just as capable and quick to bully and belittle people as 20something college students are. In my case, someone who had a considerable amount of power over my life humiliated and harassed me, and the toll it had on my mental health was incredibly negative. I found a way to remove myself from this person's influence my senior year, but the three previous years proved to be difficult to cope with because of the abuse I was facing. I was too frightened and unaware of my rights to know I could stop the bullying by informing human resources or the university's advocates.

I felt trapped. I needed the job badly, but I was feeling my life and my grades spiral down. After I found the courage to finally leave my job, I faced criticism from people for not staying with my job, during a time when many went without work, and was accused of being "lazy", "irresponsible" and "entitled". If you are faced with similar rhetoric in a situation like mine, it is best to explain, either through a letter, or through whatever communication you find most comfortable, that to leave a job where you are being belittled and abused is not cowardice. It takes great bravery to do what is best for your own mental health. Any situation which is detrimental to your mental health should be treated the same, if you have the chance to walk away from it, do so.

But after I quit, the negative impact didn't go away. I still had nightmares and anxiety troubles related to my job. I never confronted the person bullying me about the illegality and general terribleness of their behavior because the thought of confronting them made me terrified, to the point where I would start crying. The unfortunate thing about the way one's mind works is that, if you have been bullied and abused before, you can often end up frightened and unable to confront a new source of bullying, because the fear of confrontation is ingrained into you. That was certainly my case. Now, it is too late for me to confront that person, but it is not too late for me to stop my nightmares and trauma over the experience. I have a new therapist now, who has experience with Autistic adults, and I am working on ensuring that I have some closure about what happened to me at work, and working on building up the mental tools necessary to ensure it doesn't happen to me again.

All in all, college, like any new experience, is going to be filled with new sources of mental health issues and troubles. This is unavoidable. But if you prepare yourself, email the health center of the university, your doctor, or another professional, preferably one who knows you whom you have a good rapport with, your mental health can be managed before anything comes up which could force you into a situation which would be inconvenient or unhealthy for you. Nothing should force you out of college, when the suffering that often accompanies mental health trouble can be avoided or dealt with on your own terms.

Safety

Samantha April Davis

I, like many other Autistic people, have difficulty judging the intent of others. Condescension can feel like approval. Patronization can feel like respect. It can become difficult to know when and who to trust. Especially now that I am an adult in college I feel that this has placed me in a certain position of vulnerability.

Protecting myself is not always an easy thing to do. I have not always been successful.

I have found some things that I am able to do which I feel help to protect me. I try to avoid paranoia—as difficult as that may be—and, as such, I do my best to follow rules which I do not feel interfere with my life. The following make me feel safer:

I avoid risky behavior such as intoxication or seclusion with those whom I have not known for at least a month or two, no matter how I feel emotionally about them. I find that my emotional barometer is much more accurate once I have settled into a relationship with someone than when I have just met them.

I watch how people treat others around them, especially what they say about others when they are not around.

People who treat others cruelly will likely treat me cruelly, even if right now they are treating me well. If they express bigoted ideas about others then they will likely hold bigoted ideas towards me.

I listen to those people in my life who have been loyal to me for a long time.

One of the hardest parts about safety, for me, is realizing that I come from an abused and bullied past. When you are used to being bullied and excluded having someone who shows affection, whatever that affection may be, can be intoxicating and irresistible. Moving into an environment where I find myself treated humanely causes difficulty with friendships and boundaries. Everyone feels like a good friend because what you had become used to as friendship is what you should have been able to expect from everyone.

I have to keep track the length of a friendship to determine whether a person is a true friend or not. Because I have such difficulty with trust and affection I often can't tell the difference emotionally between someone who feels a strong relationship with me and someone who merely likes me around sometimes so I must use this instead to help gauge how strong our relationship is. Also, sometimes I ask what they think of our friendship.

Finally, I understand that everything is a risk. A life lived without risk is a life lived with out experience, discovery, and richness. Understand what you are doing. Understand the reality of the risk you place yourself under.

When you can accept that risk: College is a wonderful, new world and it would be a shame to miss out.

Advocacy

Leah Jane Grantham

When I first came to college, the best way to describe myself would have been, "directionless". I was uncertain about much of my life; I was undecided on a major, going from Journalism to Japanese to Asian Studies, undecided on a vocation post-college, and on what I wanted out of my college experience. All I knew is that I came to college because I had an almost fanatical love of learning, reading, and discourse, and I wished to participate in it as much as humanly possible.

I had taken Japanese in high school, and had an interest in continuing these studies, but was unsure what I could gain from it, apart from the pleasure of learning a new language and watching *Princess Mononoke* without the subtitles on. In a moment of spirited curiosity, I emailed the head of the Japanese department, who has grown to be a mentor and guide in life since coming to UM, and asked her about my options. She told me about the numerous fields open to me, such as security, governmental work, academics, and other such endeavors. Truthfully though, I still felt floating and listless, and wondered if I would end up in life as a hapless post-doc, devoted to research but never rising to the occasion.

Along with this career advice, she gave me a book that changed my life: David Suzuki and Keibo Oiwa's *The Other Japan: Voices from Beyond the Mainstream*. It was a book detailing the experiences of ethnic minorities in Japan, and it opened my eyes to the great injustices faced by those who did not fit in or conform, an experience I could strongly relate to. Stories about the horrors of institutionalized discrimination, ignorant prejudice, and the damnation of dismissive attitudes were the catalyst that launched me out of my banal student's existence. I devoted myself to my studies, hoping to one day undo the injustices I had until recently been ignorant to. I delved into books like *Our Land Was A Forest: An Ainu Memoir*, and *Multiethnic Japan* to educate myself.

Reading such books gave me a vision for my future that was crystallizing: I would do all in my power to work towards an egalitarian future, a future where environmental stewardship and freedom for all was expected, not hoped for. I expected more from my future. It would be a long ways away before I could apply this knowledge to the field though. I was devoted to causes overseas, but remained oblivious to the sad discriminatory practices and horrors right outside my own door.

That remained the norm until I was invited to participate in a pilot project on violence against people with disabilities. It was on this project that I learned some grim and unacceptable truths about the lives of people with disabilities in Montana. Stories of unspeakable pain, abuse, humiliation, and exclusion, leaving people with disabilities vulnerable and unable to live their lives to the fullest, or even at bare minimum. It all came to a head upon the discovery that at a local high school, a young autistic boy had been forced to drop out due to the bullying of his classmates. It added to the pain of stories I already knew, such as a good autistic friend of mine being bullied until he sustained permanent hair loss from the stress of the experience. "What," I said to myself, "Is the good of me working towards a brighter future for the people of Japan, when I can't even manage to help people like me, whose experiences, disabilities, and troubles are my own?"

At that point, I couldn't even help myself. I was experiencing bullying as well, not from my age-mates, but from my elders, people who I worked with whom I thought were supposed to respect me, but used their positions of power over me to berate and upset me to tears on a regular basis. After four years of contending with such conduct, I ended up leaving the workplace where it was occurring, and it was there that I found the greatest group for honing my activism: The Alliance for Disability and Students on my campus. I became their secretary, since they were in need of a work study. Around the same time, I began working on a blog. I felt it was necessary to combat stereotypes about the helplessness and futility of living with autism by showing the world my life with autism.

Along with my work on the Pilot Project, my blog and my work with ADSUM (Alliance for Disability and Students at the University of Montana) proved to be humbling and character-building experiences. I learned a lot about my own strengths, limitations, and false assumptions.

Disability advocacy is probably the single best area for an autistic person to engage in advocacy at first. You will learn a lot not only about what to do when faced with a difficult situation or a close-minded person yourself, but you will learn about the experiences and problems faced by other people with various other disabilities. Personally, I found it empowering to bond with people of other disabilities and share stories about how people perceived us based on our disabilities. It was heartening, but also provided much laughter and many new friends, especially because people with other disabilities were willing to accept behavior which other people charitably thought of as idiosyncrasies or "tics" at best, or "weird habits" or "freak rituals" at worse.

But there is another area of advocacy that is not often considered; that within your special interest, like me with my passion for Asian Law. Your special interest can take on a form of advocacy, if you are a creative thinker and can come up with ways to turn your interests into social justice. One of my autistic friends does this by taking her interest in geography and geology to work on local watershed projects, urban demonstration (Sustainable living) projects, and environmentalism. Another uses a passion for poetry to write poems about human rights. It not only strengthens you as a disabled person to fight for your rights and the rights of others, it's a way of giving a great gift to future autistic adults. You are providing them with a path to follow which was previously unavailable or not visible from their vantage point.

Ableism Awareness

Amanda Vivian

> "Sometimes you have to lie but to yourself you must always tell the truth."
>
> - Harriet the Spy

There's a lot of talk about "autism awareness," but most people I know are aware that autism exists. A lot of people don't even know the word ableism or have an understanding of the concept. (Ableism means discrimination on the basis of disability.) Of course, just because someone isn't aware of something doesn't mean they can't support it. Ableism can be unconscious and invisible. It's kind of like how homophobia and transphobia can lead to prejudice against people who don't conform to gender stereotypes, whether or not a person is labeled as gay or trans. The prevalence of ableism in our society means that certain qualities and behaviors are stigmatized without anyone really thinking about why.

Well, this is all very interesting, but what does it have to do with college? Everything. Ableism Awareness may not relate to college specifically, but it has everything to do with growing up with an invisible disability.

What is an Invisible Disability?

Some people would say that some disabilities are invisible and other disabilities are visible, and this is an objective difference between kinds of disabilities. But I would say that most disabilities could be seen if the person doing the seeing naturally expects that some of the people they meet will have disabilities. You might not know everything about the disability, but you can often see if someone has trouble doing certain things, has chronic physical or emotional pain, or is different in some other way.

There are a few things that are heavily associated with disability in the public imagination, such as being in a wheelchair or not being able to speak. But someone who is not aware of issues of disability will probably misjudge wheelchair users and nonspeaking people just as they misjudge the disabled people whom they perceive as non-disabled. The fact that they perceive some of these people as disabled and some of them as non- disabled doesn't mean that they are seeing any of these people as they really are. (For example, a lot of people make assumptions about the awareness of people who cannot talk.)

The truth is, though, that just as people don't really see the disability of someone who they read as disabled, they don't really *not* see the disability of someone who they read as non-disabled. Certain qualities are stigmatized because they are common qualities for a disabled person to have; so, a disabled person ends up being stigmatized for having those qualities, without anyone consciously thinking, "That person is disabled." Also, the prevalence of ableism leads to narrow ideas about what abilities, feelings, and experiences it is possible for a person to have; this type of narrow-mindedness can also be seen as ableist, and affects disabled people negatively whether they are perceived as disabled or not.

So maybe instead of saying that some Autistic people grow up with invisible disabilities, it's better to say that all Autistic people grow up with invisible ableism.

What about the type of disability that people mean when they say "visible disability?"

I can't write as well about the experiences of Autistic people who are always perceived as disabled, for example people who don't speak. This isn't what I know firsthand. I would guess that in some cases, "visibly disabled" Autistic people might be more aware of experiencing ableism than "invisibly disabled" Autistic people are. But a lot of the time, when someone experiences ableism and complains about it, other people will tell them that the way they were treated was only natural and that if it wasn't intended to be cruel, it isn't a problem. No matter what their disability—or the details of the ableism occurring—the person experiencing ableism can end up feeling like what happened is simply ordinary, and is what someone with a disability will inherently have to face. This can lead to self-hatred and a tendency to blame harmless features of the disability for other people's behavior.

What can you do?

In a movie where the villain is a ghost, sometimes the characters have to get special glasses that enable them to see ghosts. In your life, the villain is ableism (well there are probably other villains because life is not a movie, but ableism is the villain we're discussing right now). You'll have to make your own special glasses for seeing ableism, so you can identify when it is the source of a problem.

I can't possibly cover all the problems ableism can cause, since I fortunately have not experienced every single one. But I will try to describe some problems my Autistic friends and I have experienced growing up, to give you an idea. These problems can be caused by internalized ableism (ableist ideas that a disabled person holds against herself or again other disabled people) or external ableism (ableist ideas that non-disabled people hold against disabled people). Or both.

Ableism can make you see neutral aspects of yourself as character flaws.

If I tried to write down all the examples of this I could think of, I would probably break my computer. But one example is that I used to be upset about the fact that I run around. When I'm thinking about something that makes me happy or upset, if I'm sitting down, I get up and start leaping around and flapping my hands. If I'm walking somewhere, I just start running and leaping instead of walking. Because of the suddenness, the style of running, and the fact that I'm not wearing exercise clothes, it's pretty obvious that I'm not going for a jog. Something unusual is happening, and like lots of people who move in unusual ways I have been made fun of because I run around.

I used to try not to run around in public places, but I would have the experience that I would unconsciously think of empty places (like parts of campus where I didn't see anyone, or empty stairwells and halls) as places where it was okay to run. I would start running. Then I would notice someone was there, or someone would come out of a room. I would immediately stop running and feel like they knew something incriminating about me.

I would also experience the feeling that someone had "caught" me, or knew something embarrassing about me, whenever anyone saw me moving in a way that might look different. This covered stimming, other repetitive movements, or walking differently from other people. When I was going to meet up with a friend, I always tried to set things up so that when they first saw me I would be sitting down and they'd have to walk towards me, instead of watching me walk towards them.

When I started college I had known that I had ASD for about five years, and I knew intellectually that a lot of the movements I made were common for people with ASD; but I still saw them as embarrassing flaws in my character.

I began to feel differently when I started making more friends who were disabled and started thinking and writing about the ableism I saw around me. I realized that since I'm Autistic, there's nothing embarrassing or even notable about the fact that I might move differently, and that moving in the way that comes naturally can be a way of expressing disability pride.

This is just one example of a way that internalized ableism can affect someone. I have a friend who sometimes can't process what people are saying, and because he grew up thinking this was an embarrassment, he instinctively plays along and pretends to understand what's going on, which snowballs until he understands less and less. You can shortchange yourself and other people by trying to hide impairments, because it's hard to fully participate when you are doing that.

Ableism can make you act like a cartoon character.

A lot of the people I know who have developmental or psychiatric disabilities have had a habit of trying to act really cute and funny in order to cover for being different, or for needing help and support in situations where a non-disabled person wouldn't need help. A lot of the time, people take something about themselves that is actually real- like being confused by sarcasm, or having severe anxiety- and emphasize it as much as possible to try to turn it into a joke and earn affection and tolerance from others.

I don't want to sound critical of people who do this. It's actually a pretty smart defense mechanism because it can keep you from getting stigmatized for things you would otherwise get stigmatized for. But there's a difference between doing this on purpose to protect yourself, and getting really locked into an exaggerated persona because it seems more dignified to be a cartoon character than to be disabled.

When I used to act like a cartoon character, I remember having very strange standards about when it was appropriate to be stimmy in front of another person or to need them to talk for me. If I was always nice and funny to someone, then it was okay for them to see that I was different and it was okay for them to help me. If I ever got in a fight with a friend or acted selfish to them, then I would feel very embarrassed if they saw me stimming because I felt I didn't act well enough to make up for being different. For me, the cartoon character thing was a problem where I felt like I had to earn the right to be different. It has been really exciting for me to realize that I don't have to apologize for my impairments and differences, or use them to amuse people. I actually feel closer with my friends and communicate better now.

If someone is in a really ableist environment, they may decide that they're going to try to be as charming and funny as possible to avoid being stigmatized for being disabled. Any choice that you make to survive is fine, as long as it doesn't hurt anyone. But I think it's important to be aware of the choice you're making and why you're making it, so you don't trick yourself into thinking that you're disguising who you are because who you are is actually wrong.

I also know some people who made friends by "performing" weirdness in a cute happy way, only to find that their friends found them undesirable when they could no longer keep it together and became less adorable and more in need of support. It's worth thinking about the kind of relationships you end up in when you are being a cartoon character, and whether they are deep enough to make up for the performance you put into them.

Ableism can cause the belief that there's only one set of abilities, feelings, and experiences that a person can have.

This belief affects the way disabled people are treated, especially disabled people who are perceived as non-disabled. For example, a lot of children with sensory problems are told that they're misbehaving and being rude when loud noises, crowds, or tight clothes upset them. A person wouldn't be considered rude if they got upset because their leg was broken, but non- disabled people don't believe that sensory issues can be truly painful and uncomfortable. Also, sometimes non-Autistic people try to tell Autistic people what they're feeling, because the Autistic person's "body language" doesn't match up, in the non-Autistic person's opinion, with the emotion that the Autistic person claims to be feeling.

Disabled people can also be accused of lying when they don't have abilities that non-disabled people expect them to have. For example, if a person can read very complicated books, non-disabled people might assume she is "smart enough" to know when someone's feelings are hurt, or figure out a complex response to a setback like missing the bus. Non-disabled people can treat you with contempt if you can't do something they believe you should be able to do, because they think that you're lying and being lazy.

When someone is making statements about your feelings or abilities, the first thing to do is realize that their statements might come from ableism, rather than being accurate conclusions based on their observations of you. You don't have to accept that someone who calls you rude, oversensitive, lazy, dishonest, etc., is actually right.

If you realize that someone is being ableist and making unfair assumptions about you, you could try to point out that they're wrong. You could explain, using examples from your life, that you consistently have a certain reaction to loud noises, or that you find it hard to do certain things. You could tell them about your disability.

Of course, this doesn't always work. Some people will just take your attempts to explain as further proof of how rude, oversensitive, lazy, and dishonest you are. All you can do is remember that their judgments don't have anything to do with you and aren't your fault.

One of the worst things that happens when a disabled person is used to having non-disabled people argue with them about their experiences, feelings, and abilities is that the person begins to believe that they are not the authority on their own experience, and that if they think they're having a certain feeling or can't do a certain task, they're just lying to themselves and should keep going. This kind of internalized ableism is really dangerous, because it can lead to a person ignoring the fact that they're sick, tired, or upset and refusing to seek help or even take a break from something stressful.

Ableism can cause the belief in "mental age."

Some people have a strong idea of how a person of a certain age should talk, move, dress, think, and feel. If someone doesn't meet their standards (and often disabled people don't), they think that the person deserves to be treated like someone who's younger than they actually are. A lot of the time, if they perceive you as being "mentally" younger than your real age, these people will think that you're immature and try to do things for you or think that you can't make your own decisions or know what you're talking about.

This belief has historically had tragic consequences. For example, disabled people have been sterilized and/or kept from having sex, because they were considered to have the "mental age" of a child and therefore not to be qualified to have sex. I don't mean to imply that everyone who patronizes someone who comes off as "young for her age" is doing something as evil as this, but it is interesting to think about how prevalent this belief is and the different results it can have on how "young-seeming" people are treated.

Ableism can cause people to treat you badly because they sense or have been informed that you are disabled.

So far I've mostly been talking about how people might treat you when they don't think of you as disabled. But obviously, people can treat you badly when they *do* think of you as disabled.

Some things they might do are:

1. Assume that you don't understand the complexity of what people are saying, and not take your opinions seriously as a result, or try to "explain" to you how you should feel about things. This is a common thing to do to Autistic people because of the stereotype that we don't understand other people's points of view.

2. Call you ableist insults like the r-word; street harassment; bullying in class or at parties, etc.

3. Assume not only that you don't understand complex statements, but also that you don't understand anything that's being said at all. (This often happens to people who are non-speaking.)

4. Believe that it's not appropriate for someone like you to be interested in having sex or a relationship.

5. Believe that they don't have to treat you as respectfully as they would treat their other friends, because you are too naive, or too desperate for acceptance, to know the difference. This can also happen in romantic and sexual relationships.

I obviously haven't listed all the ableist things someone could possibly do. It's also the case that some of these things are worse than others and you might have different reactions to different things on the list. If a friend is talking down to you or explaining everything to you, you might choose to remain friends to them and try to ignore their behavior or educate them on what is wrong with it. If a sexual partner is abusing you because they think that you won't be able to tell what they're doing is wrong, you would probably want to end the relationship.

You can't always just stand up to someone and tell him or her to change his or her behavior. Obviously, sometimes you can. For example, if someone is your friend, you could have a talk with him or her about how they need to respect your feelings as being real, even if your feelings don't make sense to them. This might make them understand their behavior in a new way, and see that the way they were acting was wrong.

Some people will not respond well to this. Even if they're supposed to be your friend, they might not respect what you have to say, and will just get annoyed (or patronizing) and deny that they did anything wrong. When this happens, you'll have to figure out if you want to be friends with a person who behaves this way, and you might conclude that you don't.

In other cases, the person who is being ableist is not your friend. For example, if a stranger is yelling at you on the street about the way you walk, it's not that likely that you're going to be able to talk to them and get them to change their behavior, and it might be dangerous to try. An acquaintance might talk to you in a patronizing way, and you don't really know them well enough to have a talk with them about why their behavior is wrong. In these cases, all you can really do to protect yourself is to try to avoid the person, and try to understand that what's happening isn't your fault.

I don't mean to imply that stopping other people's ableism isn't important. But one of the biggest things that ableism goggles can give you is the ability to accept parts of yourself that you saw as unacceptable because you associated them with disability.

Professors

Samantha April Davis

Two years ago my brain changed. I stopped being able to control my motor impulses. I started to convulse and shudder. My voice began to make noises, even bark. It was difficult to pay attention in class, even more difficult to take a test. I needed help, yet, because of the newness of my condition I had never been diagnosed and had no paperwork to turn into the disability office. They told me they couldn't help me.

I turned to my professors. They knew me. They could see the difficulties that I was trying to navigate. They knew I needed help. When I approached them they worked with me and found ways in  which I could be accommodated, including finding me private rooms in which I could take my tests. All without having to work through the disability office, which finally offered me official accommodations right before finals. Truth is, I don't have my autism registered with the disability office either.

How am I able to get professors to work with me? I make sure they know me. I engage them and speak with them at every opportunity. I communicate my needs, even when my needs are not strictly disability related. I make sure they notice me and I work hard.

Approaching a professor can often be a very nerve wracking ordeal. Even many neurotypical students feel anxiety in a professor's office. One thing that helps me greatly is that I make a habit of talking to a given professor at least once a week, usually for a minute or two after class. Once I get into this routine it starts to become normal and, like many things in my life, it gains certain inertia. After years of doing this I have gotten to the point where it is significantly easier to approach a professor. It is still nerve-wracking when I need help or an accommodation but—where it would have been impossible before—it is now something I am able to handle.

Others might have trouble speaking to professors at all. Yet, with the importance of face-to-face contact with a professor it is very unwise to avoid contact entirely.  Fortunately, interactions between yourself and your professor are under no requirement to be normative in any way. Writing a note and then handing it to the professor when you approach them during their office or after class and waiting for them to read it is a very good way of handling the stress of having to speak while at the same time communicating with them and giving the professor ample opportunity to learn who you are. Consider explaining on your first note why you are communicating in this way. The professor will remember you and will appreciate that you take your education seriously enough to overcome the barriers required to communicate with them.

Do not use email to get to know your professor. Email does have its place such as when you need to communicate something quickly with a professor whom you already know or when it is important and you need to reduce the risk of executive function failure. Nonetheless, professors and other faculty tend to receive at least 20 to 30 emails every single day. They may get your message but they will not remember your name, much less associate your name with your face and who you are as an individual. If you must communicate via written communication, hand deliver a note in an envelope from your hand to the professor's hand. An unusual envelope, such as one with graphics, one with an unusual color, or one with a wax seal will stand out and will prime their memory as to who gave them the letter when they go to open it. Never rely on a professor remembering your name.

Do not wait until you have a pressing concern before seeing your professor! When you do need help things can get very stressful. In fact, asking for accommodations for a disability can be a highly embarrassing or even humiliating experience for many. It is important to know how to ask. Firstly, it is not always important to frame all your needs as accessibility issues, even when they are. This does not mean that the professor cannot know you are disabled merely that you do not always refer to the disability when you are asking for accommodations. Even though autism affects your needs many of the things that are needed because of your neurotype are also similar to things which neurotypicals need. Because your professor is likely neurotypical, or at least likely identifies as such, framing your request in a way they can identify with will help them understand that you are in legitimate need. When your needs are radically different, it may require framing with regards to autism but it never hurts to try first. You can always tell them why you need it if questioned. You are, like many other students, a student who sometimes struggles and sometimes needs help from their professors. The reasons why you may need this help and exactly what kind of help you need may vary slightly but the principle remains the same. Professors are used to this. They understand that students need help and, the vast majority of the time, they want to provide you with that help. Especially when they understand your dedication and situation they will be very willing to give you whatever support is reasonable and required for your success. After all, your professor had to complete college, too, and understands that sometimes, neurotypical or not, students need a bit of help.

Discussing Disability with Friends and in Class

Amanda Vivian

So you're in your psychology class, and this week you're studying autism. The professor starts off by asking, "Does anyone have a family member with autism?"

You wonder, does "self" count as a family member?

Or your friend comes back from Thanksgiving, which they spent with their disabled cousin. "I was uncomfortable. Handicapped people kind of freak me out."

<u>Awkward Turtle</u>

A lot of college students like to make a hand gesture called "awkward turtle" to express discomfort in awkward situations. It's the obvious response when someone starts talking about disability as though there are no disabled people in the room. You put your hands on top of each other and wiggle your thumbs back and forth. It's supposed to look like a turtle swimming around.

Making an awkward turtle under the table can make you feel better when someone says something like this, but you might find yourself wanting to say a bit more.

If your friend makes a comment about disability that you don't agree with or that you think is offensive, it can be challenging to figure out how to respond. The challenge is doubled when the other person either doesn't know that you're Autistic, or knows but "doesn't think of you that way." Now you have not one but two tasks:

    a. figure out how to express your disagreement, and

    b. disclose (or remind) that you are Autistic.

Reminding People That You Are Autistic

A lot of people feel anxious when delivering a coming out speech ("There's something important you should know about me. I'm Autistic"). A coming out speech can also cause the conversation to feel very serious, and can be a hindrance if you were hoping to casually make a point and then move on.

However, sometimes the person you're talking to knows the parts but not the whole. They may know that you have a certain history or diagnosis, but they haven't made the connection that you consider yourself disabled or Autistic.

That makes the situation a little easier. Instead of telling them totally new information, you're reminding them of something they've heard before. Often you can make your point just by inserting "I'm Autistic" or "I'm disabled" into your opinion, as if you are just restating something that you're sure they already understand.

One thing to be aware of is that some people may correct you because they perceive words like "disabled" as negative, and think that you are "putting yourself down" by using the word. So be prepared to explain that for you, the word is just a description, and you are not insulting yourself by using it. (Some people may tell you that you "aren't Autistic" or "aren't disabled" as a way of trying to win an argument. These people are jerks and you don't have to respond when they say those things.)

Fake-Reminding

If you find it fairly easy and comfortable to remind someone that you're Autistic, and fairly difficult to make a coming out speech about being Autistic, you may want to adopt the practice of "fake-reminding." This is when you're talking to someone who doesn't know you're Autistic, but you casually mention it as if you think they already know. This isn't lying because it doesn't affect the content of what you're saying; it just makes it easier to say.

The problem with coming out speeches, besides the fact that they can make you nervous, is that you often feel like you have to share your whole personal and medical history in order to explain your identity. If you assume someone already knows, you can be much more brief; and if the person is really curious about trivia like when you were diagnosed, they have to be the one to bring it up.

Another advantage of stating your identity concisely is that you seem more secure in that identity. So the person you're talking to is a little less likely to think you are anxious and try to comfort you with, "You're not really disabled, stop putting yourself down!"

Even when you are really coming out, it's often less awkward for everyone if you can relate it to the topic at hand instead of making what you're saying the new topic of conversation. However, be aware that all these methods of disclosure have a drawback that is the same as the benefit—because they are not dramatic, they can go right over some people's heads.

<u>Coming Out Noisly</u>

There are some people who are so closed off to the idea that they could be talking to someone who has a disability, especially a disability as stigmatized as autism, that they won't pick up on you mentioning that you have it.

Subsets of people exist who literally don't hear perfectly clear coming-out statements, or reconfigure them in their heads as a different sentence. For example, they might hear the sentence, "I have autism," as "I've worked with kids who have autism." (Real example.)

When this happens, it's pretty confusing for the person who's trying to come out. You made references. When that didn't work, you screwed up your courage and said something very unambiguous. But the other person still doesn't understand the basic idea of what you are saying.

What can you do?

If you think that the person isn't taking in what you're saying, you can always say it again, and ask them to repeat back to you what they think you're saying. You could also ask them what they think of what you said so you can counter any doubts they have about you being Autistic (for example, some people seem to get confused and think that someone who's Autistic can't have friends or look anyone in the eye).

Being this aggressive about making sure someone knows you're Autistic can be stressful for some people, because it can bring up insecurities many Autistic people have about talking too much, being repetitive, over

explaining things, or not knowing what other people are thinking. If this kind of conversation would make you anxious, another idea is to write the person an email, Facebook message, or letter explaining that you're Autistic. It's a bit harder for someone to ignore what you're saying if they're reading it instead of hearing it.

If Things Go Badly With A Friend

If you tell your friend that they offended you or made you feel invisible, this can turn into a fight. Your friend may cry or become angry and say that you're being too politically correct or that you're being mean to them.

Some people get upset when their behavior or opinions are criticized, no matter how polite the person criticizing them was. So don't assume just because your friend is upset that you did 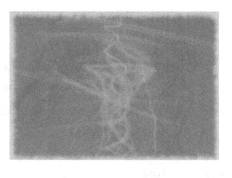 something wrong. Maybe you could summarize the conversation to another friend and ask if they think you were being too harsh. It helps if this other friend is someone who understands and is tolerant of your feelings about disability, so that they aren't confused or biased by the content of the conversation. If you end up feeling that you were being mean, you may want to apologize for the way you expressed your opinions, though not your opinions themselves.

A conflict that is based on your identity, and your and your friend's values, can be hard to dissect afterward. The surface conflict—your and your friend's different opinions about disability—get mixed in with a lot of other things, like whether you or your friend was being mean, your and your friend's emotional states during the conversation, your personal investment as a disabled person, and conflicts that you and your friend have had about other things. Even if you come to the conclusion that you weren't mean to your friend, you might still feel like you have caused a problem by calling your friend out on something that offended you.

Things may change. Your friend may become more accepting of your point of view, or even come to share it. But this may not happen; disability may become an issue that causes a conflict whenever you and your friend talk about it.

If you have a friend who says things that upset you, and you learn that you can't talk to them about it without having a fight, you will have to decide what that means for your friendship. Many people are friends with someone who acts or thinks in a way that they disagree with. Other people are bothered by being friends with someone whose views they find offensive, but will put up with it if they've been friends for a long time or have a lot of mutual friends.

But this might not be the case for you. You might end up feeling that it's not worth it to be friends with someone who has said what this person said. You might not get a choice, either, if the person is mad enough at you for calling them out; they might decide to stop being friends with you. If you lose a friend due to speaking up about disability, it's important that you understand it isn't your fault. You have no responsibility to keep quiet when someone who's supposed to care about you is insulting a group that you belong to.

In Class

So far I have talked about how to discuss these issues with a friend or acquaintance in an informal setting. But you may also have cause to discuss them in class, and by sharing a perspective that is often ignored you can make a difference to how your classmates think about disability and autism.

Talking about disability in class can be easier than talking about it to friends, because usually you don't know the people in your class very well. But it's harder for the same reason. The environment is also a bit more structured and formal—you're often expected to express your opinion in one or two comments, instead of being able to say more things as you think of them.

This can be easier for some people and harder for others.

Do's And Don'ts

(suggestions, not hard and fast rules)

DO know what you're getting into. No one is a bad person if they decide that they don't want to talk about their beliefs, or their personal disability experience, in front of the entire class. If talking about this is going to make you so nervous that you have a shutdown or a panic attack, then don't feel obligated to do it. Also, think about whether you're taking risks that are safe to take. For example, if you want to tell your professor that they said something offensive, consider whether the professor is likely to get angry, and how important your grade in the class is.

DO talk about how you feel. For example, instead of saying, "It's wrong for you to say that autism is a tragedy," you could say, "As someone who has autism, I don't really agree with the use of the word tragedy—things can be really hard, but I don't consider my life a tragedy. To me tragedy implies a situation that's completely bleak, but for me, and really for anyone with a disability, just because things are hard doesn't mean that there won't be things you can enjoy about life or things you'll be able to do." By talking about your feelings, you can express a very similar opinion while making it sound less like an attack. Also, if your opinion is something your classmates and professor haven't heard before, you can make it easier for them to relate to.

DO try to stay on topic. If you just straight out say, "Excuse me, this is offensive," people are more likely to be angry and perceive you as "having an agenda." A lot of the time, you can stick to the general tone of the conversation while still expressing yourself. For example, if you read a book for a literature class that you think is ableist, you could bring up the poor treatment of disability as something that detracts from the quality of the book, or you could discuss ableism as a theme in the book. Something that's kind of cool about this approach is that it treats the disabled/anti-ableist point of view as just another point of view that can be discussed—which can help normalize disability and dissolve the "no disabled people in the room" assumption.

DO indicate that you're not alone. Many people are not aware of Autistic self- advocacy or disability rights in general, so the views you express may seem really strange. Your classmates and professors may think that you're talking without thinking or trying to be outrageous. So it can help to say, "A lot of people in the disability community say..." or "My Autistic friends and I think..." While people still may disagree with you, they will understand that you've thought about these issues before and you're not the only one who has your beliefs.

DON'T necessarily feel that you have to say you're disabled or Autistic. Obviously, in some cases it helps support what you're saying, but other times you can make your point without mentioning your identity. The reverse is also true:

DON'T feel that you have to start arguing or stating opinions, when just disclosing makes the point well enough. If your professor asks, "Does anyone have a family member with autism?" and you reply, "I have autism and so does my best friend," this shows what was wrong with your professor's question.

DON'T feel obligated to answer personal questions. If someone responds to your admission that you're Autistic by asking for examples of what your disability is like, this may make you uncomfortable or be a confusing question to answer. Also, some people may derail the conversation by arguing with you about your examples. So if someone starts asking you questions like this, feel free to say that it makes you uncomfortable and you don't think it's relevant.

DON'T let people make you feel bad with responses like, "This is obviously an emotional subject for you," or, "You seem to have a personal investment." Sometimes people will say things like this as a way of implying that your opinion is biased. But having a personal investment just means that you've probably thought and learned a lot about the issues you're discussing, which makes you more qualified to talk about them, not less.

DON'T feel guilty that your behavior might fit into stereotypes about Autistic people, like changing the conversation to your favorite topic, or being insensitive to other people's views. Don't get me wrong—there's value in noticing when stereotypes could hurt you. But there's a difference between being aware of potential discrimination, and actually being mad at yourself because you said something that someone could interpret that way. Non-Autistic people don't have to think, "Oh no, I was acting so non- Autistic," because they shot down someone's opinion or went on and on about the same thing. You should have the same right.

<u>No Disclosure</u>

So far, these suggestions have been aimed at a reader who is willing to come out as Autistic, if it's necessary and they can find a comfortable way to do so. Of course, you may not be such a reader. You may have decided that you don't want anyone at college to know you're Autistic.

There are drawbacks to keeping this kind of secret, but you're the only person who can judge whether it is the right decision for you. I hope that some of the tactics I listed are ones that you can still use, or adapt for yourself, without coming out. One thing that sometimes works is to talk about the experiences of a (real or imaginary) Autistic friend. Also, in some situations you can share your opinion without having to talk about anyone's personal experience.

Good luck.

Social Activities

Steven Kapp

Colleges offer many social opportunities. They generally have student organizations, with up to several hundred to choose from depending on the size of the college, and the option to start your own. You may be able to find a list of student organizations online or in a student government office on campus. You might also meet people promoting their organizations at specially designated events like freshman orientation or during the beginning of the term, or perhaps see people standing or sitting at a table outside at other points advertising their organization.

I suggest joining at least one organization and determining what you think of the members and activities and how it fits your schedule before deciding whether to drop it or add others. I probably became too involved in my first semester in college before I had time to adjust to the transition, joining the marching band, student newspaper, building government of my dorm, and a religious organization. Also, the band and building government did not provide a good fit because I had no background or particular interest in music or student government. I had unrealistic ambitions about making the most of the college experience, since no one can do everything; we should do what makes sense for us.

For that matter, you should not do anything illegal or against your will, even if most students do the activity or you think they do, such as drinking alcohol or smoking recreational drugs. You are free to decide not to go to parties as well, especially if they are in students' rooms or houses (rather than, for example, a public building on campus). Parties can be loud and overstimulating, and might have peer pressure, wild, and illegal activities.

Student organizations vary widely in level of commitment and type. One type you might consider is service organizations in which you help people or the environment in the community, because they offer a good chance to improve your surroundings in a possibly structured way, while allowing you a social – and perhaps physical – outlet. One community service organization I joined enabled me to co-teach mini-courses in schools in the local underprivileged area. Another, my college's chapter of Best Buddies International, paired me in a one-to-one relationship with a student with an intellectual disability; I hung out with him when I visited his school and participated in group events with other Best Buddies members. These experiences helped prepare me, and helped me decide, to join a PhD program in education to help other autistics and people with disabilities. I also gained leadership experience as a student officer in organizations like Best Buddies, which, like some of the organizations themselves, may feel more like a side project or work you enjoy than a social activity.

You also might enjoy campus events. You might go with a peer or group you met in class or a student organization. Going alone can be fun too and may be easier, for example if others have schedule conflicts or if planning would take too long. I went by myself many times and sometimes had conversations and became acquainted with others nearby. Your college might have artistic and cultural events like plays and concerts, entertainment such as sports games, or open lectures by visitors.

Despite all these opportunities, you might feel that other students, faculty, or staff do not give you the respect or support you or others with disabilities deserve; you might decide to become actively involved in self-advocacy beyond getting personal accommodations or services. Those services, and disability awareness and attitudes, vary at different colleges. Generally, although colleges are often relatively progressive and promote civil rights for other groups, they are less likely to embrace people with disabilities as making up a minority group. Disabilities like autism often carry stigma so students with disabilities may not self-disclose to get the understanding, acceptance, and support we need.

Fortunately, I found out in my sophomore year that the neurodiversity and disability rights movements encourage the self-empowerment of and social justice for people with disabilities. In my sophomore year I tried to work with the director of student programming to create a student administration on disability, but she said it would first need student disability organizations. Sadly my college, although it is the second largest private university in the United States, had no student organization for its own students with disabilities. In my junior year I started a student organization about autism, and had about as many panelists (mainly autistic students from other colleges) as attendees, or about six people. Hardly anyone helped me with the organization's founding or event, so after planning, publicizing, and coordinating the panel, I realized I had too much work as one person. Thankfully, in my senior year I spoke with a candidate for student government vice president about the need for a Disability Awareness Week, and this eventually led to a wheelchair basketball event in my final semester. The following year, the college had its first annual Disability Awareness Week.

The message I take from this is that autistic or disability self-advocacy helps to advance our rights and does important work but can require a great commitment and skills as a student leader that you might not have when you start college. If your college already has a group like the Autistic Self Advocacy Network, you can become active without needing to lead right away. In general though, self-advocacy requires networking and communication skills that can be difficult. Nevertheless, they can help you advocate on behalf of others so that they can build adaptive skills and have a higher quality of life.

Social Issues

Alexander Eveleth

A large part of your experience at college will be interacting with your fellow students in a variety of situations. Cooperating with studying or work for classes is one example, as are mealtimes and campus clubs or organizations. You can't get through college *without* having a lot of interactions with other students. But that doesn't have to be a problem. I'm focusing here on my own personal experience, based on going from high school to college and knowing nobody at the new campus.

Interacting with peers is often one of the difficult bits in high school (you'll note that it's hard for everybody, even non-autistic people), but college is a clean slate. Generally speaking, high school doesn't follow you when you leave it—thankfully—which gives you all kinds of new opportunities. I'm not saying to go overboard and totally reinvent yourself (I remember reading about a guy who found himself faced with explaining to his new girlfriend that he was not, as he had been claiming, Australian, and in fact hailed from suburban New Jersey), but colleges are big enough that none of the more unpleasant aspects of high school need to follow you between campuses. In college, much more so than high school, it's possible, and even easy, to find a circle of people you share interests with.

That said, don't be afraid to branch out past your traditional zone of interests. Join clubs and organizations you find interesting—you'll discover a lot of people to spend some time with.

And of course, if you really do find yourself more comfortable in the library with a stack of books than you do eating lunch with a table of people, do that. Living on your own often equals freedom to choose your leisure and stick to the things you enjoy.

But even if you do decide to make the library your home away from home and spend more time with your books and laptop than with other students (and there can be a bright future in academic or professional life for you) you'll have to spend at least some time interacting with others. Especially since the end of high school doesn't mean the end of group work and class projects.

Overall, and I know this is far easier said than done, you'll find yourself happiest, socially, when you stop worrying.

When I came to college, I was determined that it would be a fresh start after being an awkward kid in high school. So all through freshman year, I was always worrying about how I was doing socially—was I being awkward? Were there things I was missing socially? What did I need to do better when I was talking to people?

But worrying about things isn't really going to make it any better. And, if you're in my age group (coming into college from high school, at seventeen or eighteen years old) you're going to find yourself at a really important junction in your life, one that's going to make a lot of difference for you based on how it all works out. Working off of my own experience, I want to give some advice on the problem of showing up to college and feeling really awkward.

Let's be frank: for me, there were very few redeeming features of elementary through high school, especially compared to college. There were plenty of times when life before college just wasn't fun at all.

College doesn't have to be that. It's big enough and new enough that almost nobody will know you there. Every time you meet somebody your first day at college it's a first impression, starting anew. At an important time in your life, *you* control how people see you. If you're worried about being awkward socially, this is your time to undo that.

A big part of any transition is finding yourself—figuring out who you are and what you're like. This takes time, and it takes experience, and exposure to a lot of new things, which college is great for. And figuring that out is how, in my experience, to stop worrying about fitting in socially. You won't be perfect. But if you're comfortable with being yourself, you'll be less nervous, about social problems and merely in general. Once you start getting a grip on who you are—and you may find it very different from what you thought you were like while you were in high school—the trick to not being nervous about yourself is to just be yourself.

Not everyone is going to like you. And nobody can really make everybody like him or herself, even if they're the most charming person in the world. Businesspeople spend millions each year on books and training seminars geared towards making other people like them. There's a whole *science* to first impressions, covering everything from what side of someone to stand on when talking so that they're more receptive to what you're saying (it's their left) to the precise duration of a handshake (one, one thousand). When

Dale Carnegie came out with *How To Win Friends and Influence People* in 1937 it sold like hotcakes. But, if nothing else, people respect confidence. Be confident about being yourself, and you won't need to worry.

When I got to college at the beginning of my freshman year, I was nervous about how people were going to see me. But I was going to a place where nobody knew who I was—I was in control of making good impressions. Not everything went my way, but I made sure I learned when it didn't.

At the end of that year, I moved out of the dorms and into a house with four friends, all people I'd met there that year at college. That summer, my family went to Europe. One afternoon in August I was walking down the street in Munich when it started to pour on me. I ducked into the first place I could, a nearby beer garden, to see if I could wait out the rain before heading back to my hostel.

I ended up spending the next four hours at that beer garden, learning the names of everybody there—it turned out one of the regulars was celebrating his birthday—and, despite the language barrier, several people bought me rounds of drinks. And there was *nothing* to worry about.

There comes a point where you have to stop worrying and, for better or worse, be yourself. Self-confidence is, itself, the biggest improvement you can make if you're concerned about your social life. And it will come with time. Being you and being confident about that, more than anything else, is the mark of social success.

Notes

Notes

Notes

Notes

Notes

Notes

Notes

CPSIA information can be obtained
at www.ICGtesting.com
Printed in the USA
LVHW051142170419
614500LV00020B/626